RIDGEFIELD LIBRARY ASSOCIATION

3 4010 10342 1714

W9-AHA-685

DATE DUE

| NOV 2 5 2005 | |
| SEP 1 4 2006 | |
| NOV 1 4 2006 | |
| NOV 2 5 2006 | |
| MAY 1 4 2007 | |
| JUL 3 1 2007 | |
| OCT 0 6 2007 | |
| AUG 1 9 2008 | |
| MAR 2 8 2022 | |

DEMCO, INC. 38-2931

WITHDRAWN

RIDGEFIELD LIBRARY
472 MAIN STREET
RIDGEFIELD, CONN. 06877

OCT 2 0 2005

GRAPHIC HISTORY

# The SALEM WITCH TRIALS

by Michael Martin
illustrated by Brian Bascle

Consultant:
Walter W. Woodward
Assistant Professor of History
University of Connecticut, Hartford

Capstone

Mankato, Minnesota

Graphic Library is published by Capstone Press,
151 Good Counsel Drive, P.O. Box 669, Mankato, Minnesota 56002.
www.capstonepress.com

Copyright © 2005 by Capstone Press. All rights reserved.
No part of this publication may be reproduced in whole or in part, or stored in a retrieval
system, or transmitted in any form or by any means, electronic, mechanical,
photocopying, recording, or otherwise, without written permission of the publisher.
For information regarding permission, write to Capstone Press,
151 Good Counsel Drive, P.O. Box 669, Dept. R, Mankato, Minnesota 56002.
Printed in the United States of America

1 2 3 4 5 6 10 09 08 07 06 05

*Library of Congress Cataloging-in-Publication Data*
Martin, Michael, 1948–
    The Salem witch trials / by Michael Martin; illustrated by Brian Bascle.
    p. cm.—(Graphic library. Graphic history)
    Includes bibliographical references and index.
    ISBN 0-7368-3847-3 (hardcover)
    ISBN 0-7368-5246-8 (paperback)
    1. Trials (Witchcraft)—Massachusetts—Salem—History—17th century—Juvenile
literature. 2. Witchcraft—Massachusetts—Salem—Juvenile literature.  I. Bascle, Brian.
II. Title. III. Series.
BF1576.M36 2005
133.4'3'097445—dc22                        2004019145

Summary: The story of the 1692 witchcraft trials in Salem, Massachusetts, told in graphic
    novel format.

**Editor's note:** Direct quotations from primary sources are indicated by a yellow background.
    Direct quotations appear on the following pages:
Pages 5, 23, from Samuel Parris' sermons, quoted in *A Delusion of Satan* by Frances Hill
    (New York: Doubleday, 1995).
Pages 6, 21, from Cotton Mather's *Memorable Providences, Relating to Witchcrafts and*
    *Possessions.*
Pages 8, 11, 12, 24, from *The Salem Witchcraft Papers*, edited by Paul Boyer and Stephen
    Nissenbaum (University of Virginia Library.
    http://etext.virginia.edu/salem/witchcraft/texts/transcripts.html)
Page 25, from Increase Mather's "Cases of Conscience Concerning Evil Spirits Personating
    Men," quoted in *Delusion of Satan* by Frances Hill (New York: Doubleday, 1995).
Page 27, from Ann Putnam's apology in 1706, quoted in *A Delusion of Satan* by Frances Hill
    (New York: Doubleday, 1995).

### Credits

**Art Director and Storyboard Artist**
Jason Knudson

**Art Director**
Heather Kindseth

**Editor**
Rebecca Glaser

### Acknowledgment

Capstone Press thanks Philip Charles
Crawford, Library Director, Essex High
School, Essex, Vermont, and columnist for
*Knowledge Quest*, for his assistance in
the preparation of this book.

# Table of Contents

CHAPTER · 1

# Strange Behavior in Salem

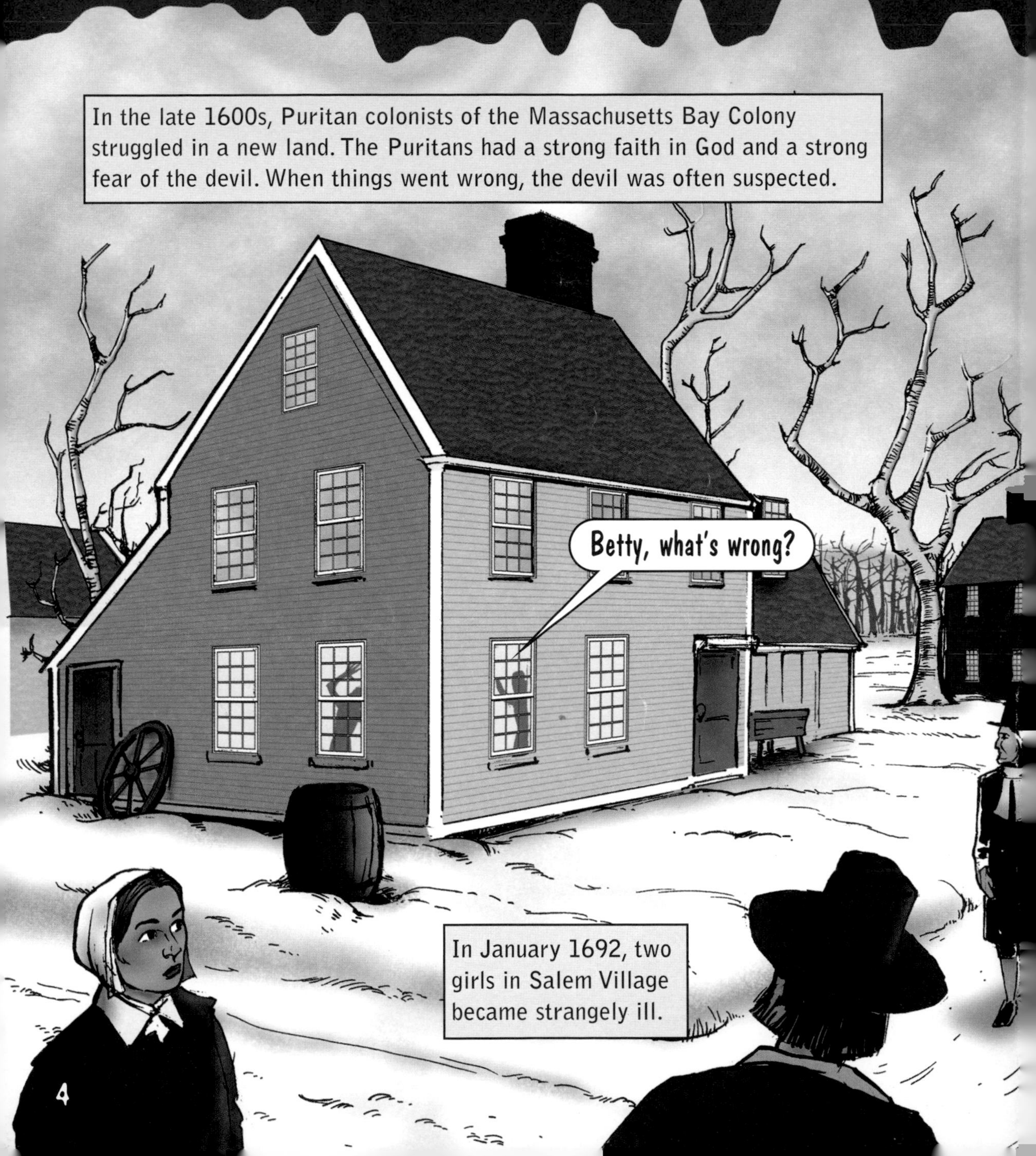
In the late 1600s, Puritan colonists of the Massachusetts Bay Colony struggled in a new land. The Puritans had a strong faith in God and a strong fear of the devil. When things went wrong, the devil was often suspected.
Betty, what's wrong?
In January 1692, two girls in Salem Village became strangely ill.

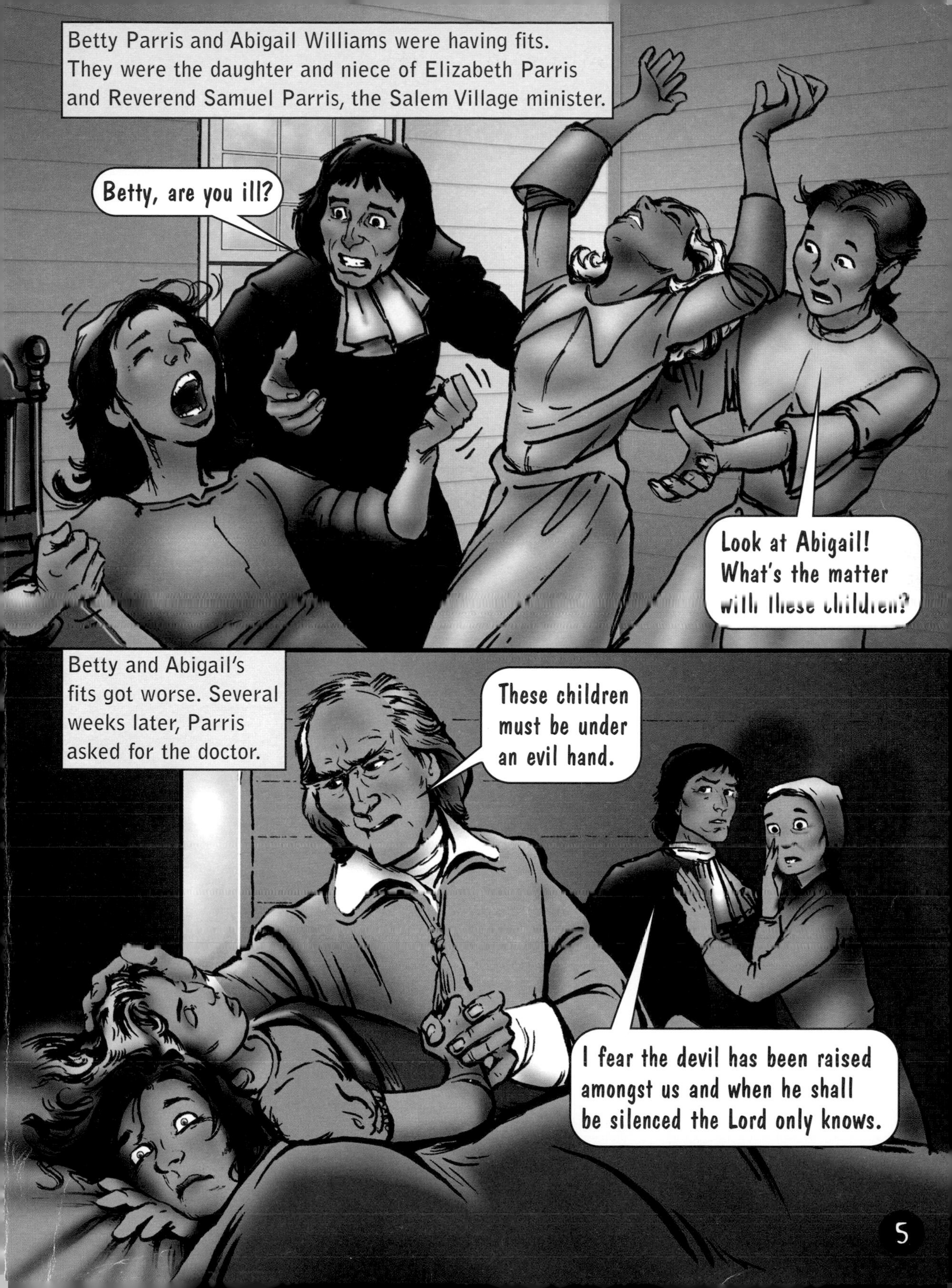
Betty Parris and Abigail Williams were having fits. They were the daughter and niece of Elizabeth Parris and Reverend Samuel Parris, the Salem Village minister.
Betty, are you ill?
Look at Abigail! What's the matter with these children?
Betty and Abigail's fits got worse. Several weeks later, Parris asked for the doctor.
These children must be under an evil hand.
I fear the devil has been raised amongst us and when he shall be silenced the Lord only knows.

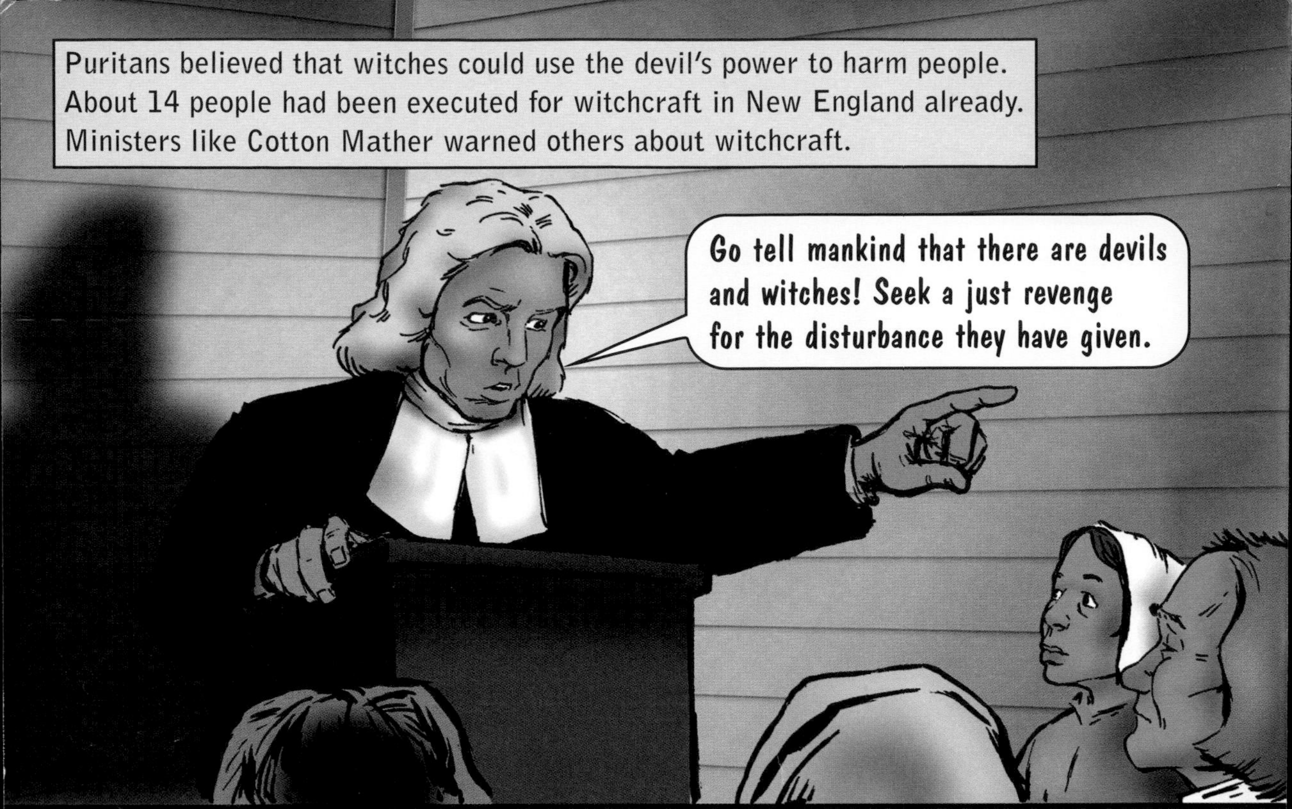
Puritans believed that witches could use the devil's power to harm people. About 14 people had been executed for witchcraft in New England already. Ministers like Cotton Mather warned others about witchcraft.
Go tell mankind that there are devils and witches! Seek a just revenge for the disturbance they have given.

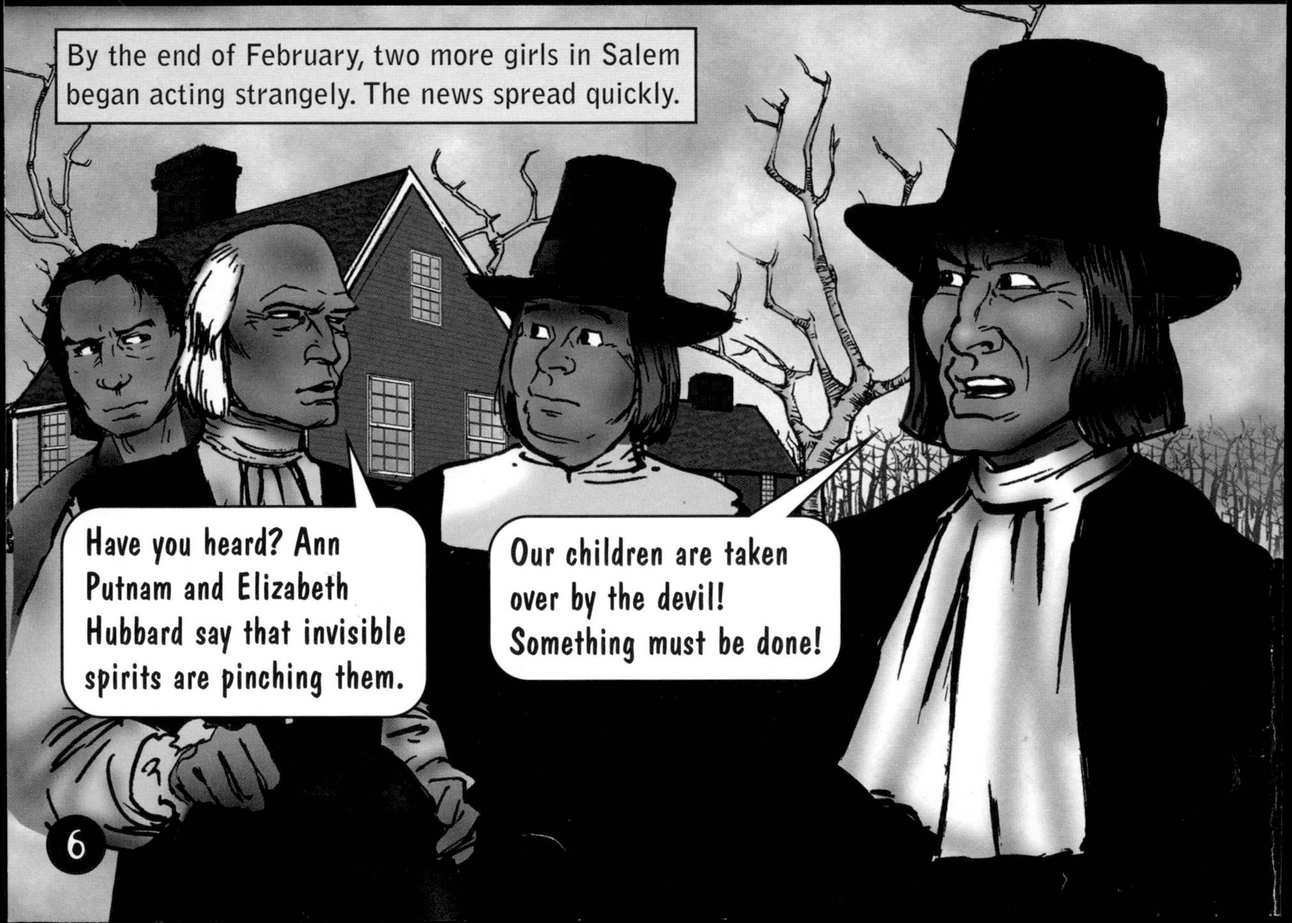
By the end of February, two more girls in Salem began acting strangely. The news spread quickly.
Have you heard? Ann Putnam and Elizabeth Hubbard say that invisible spirits are pinching them.
Our children are taken over by the devil! Something must be done!

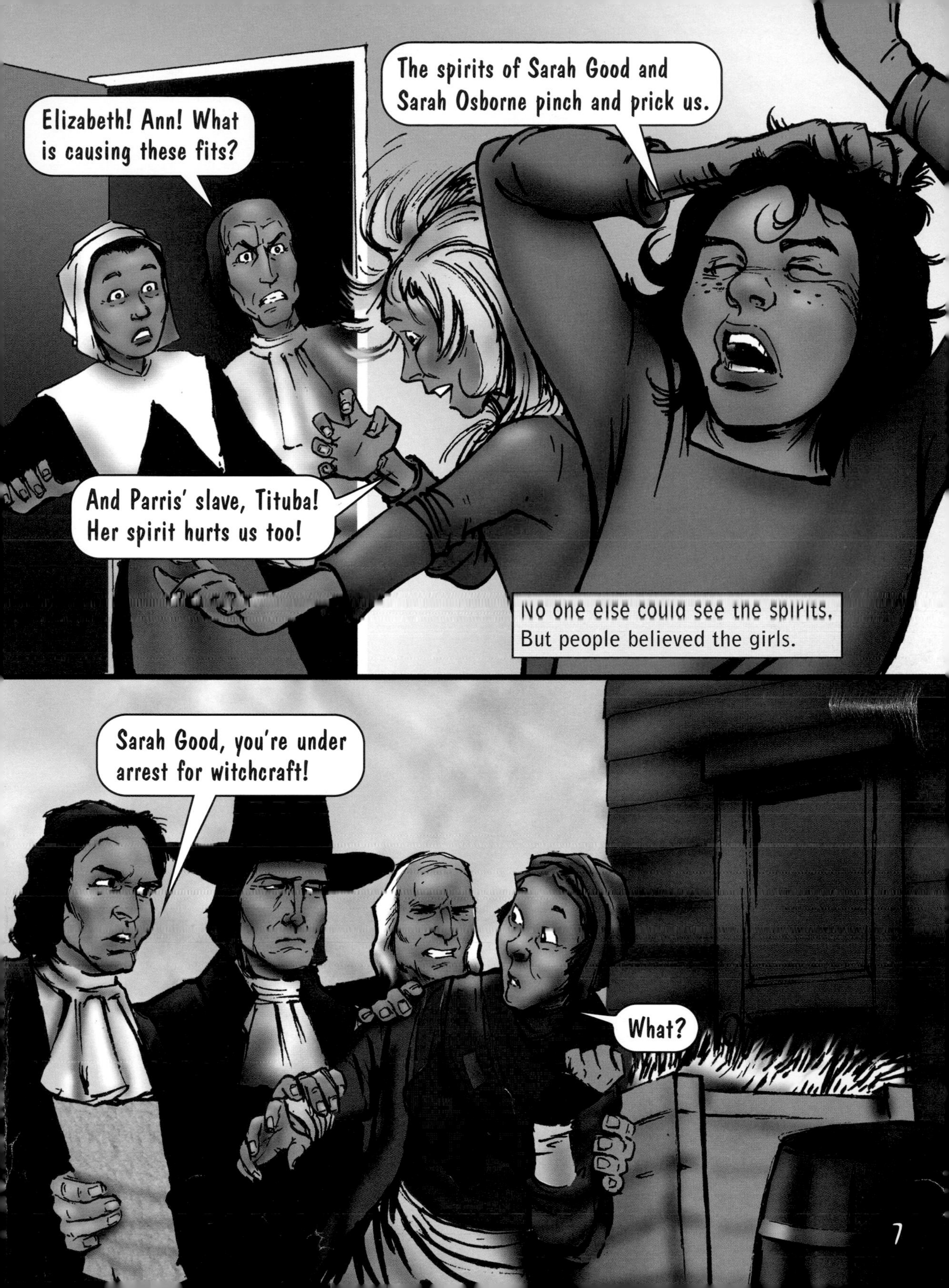
Elizabeth! Ann! What is causing these fits?
The spirits of Sarah Good and Sarah Osborne pinch and prick us.
And Parris' slave, Tituba! Her spirit hurts us too!
No one else could see the spirits. But people believed the girls.
Sarah Good, you're under arrest for witchcraft!
What?

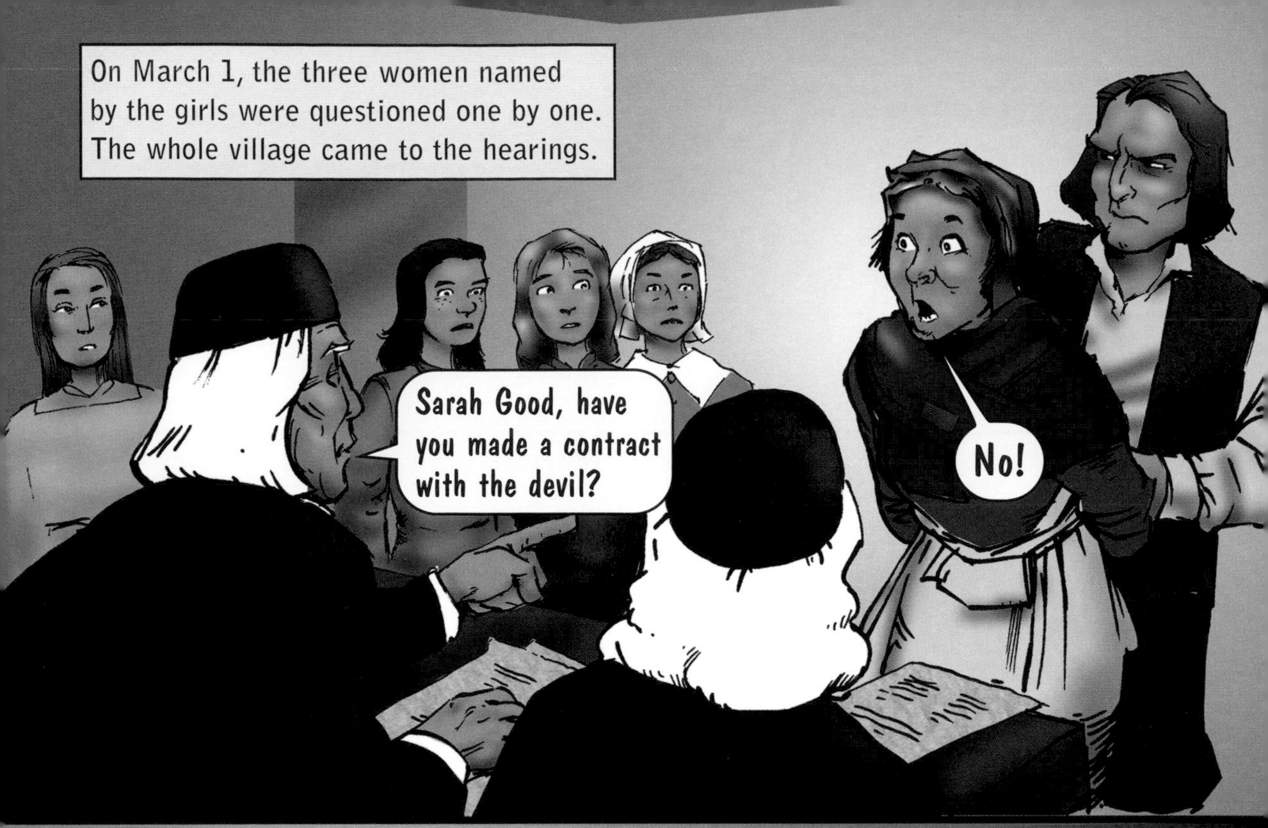
On March 1, the three women named by the girls were questioned one by one. The whole village came to the hearings.
Sarah Good, have you made a contract with the devil?
No!

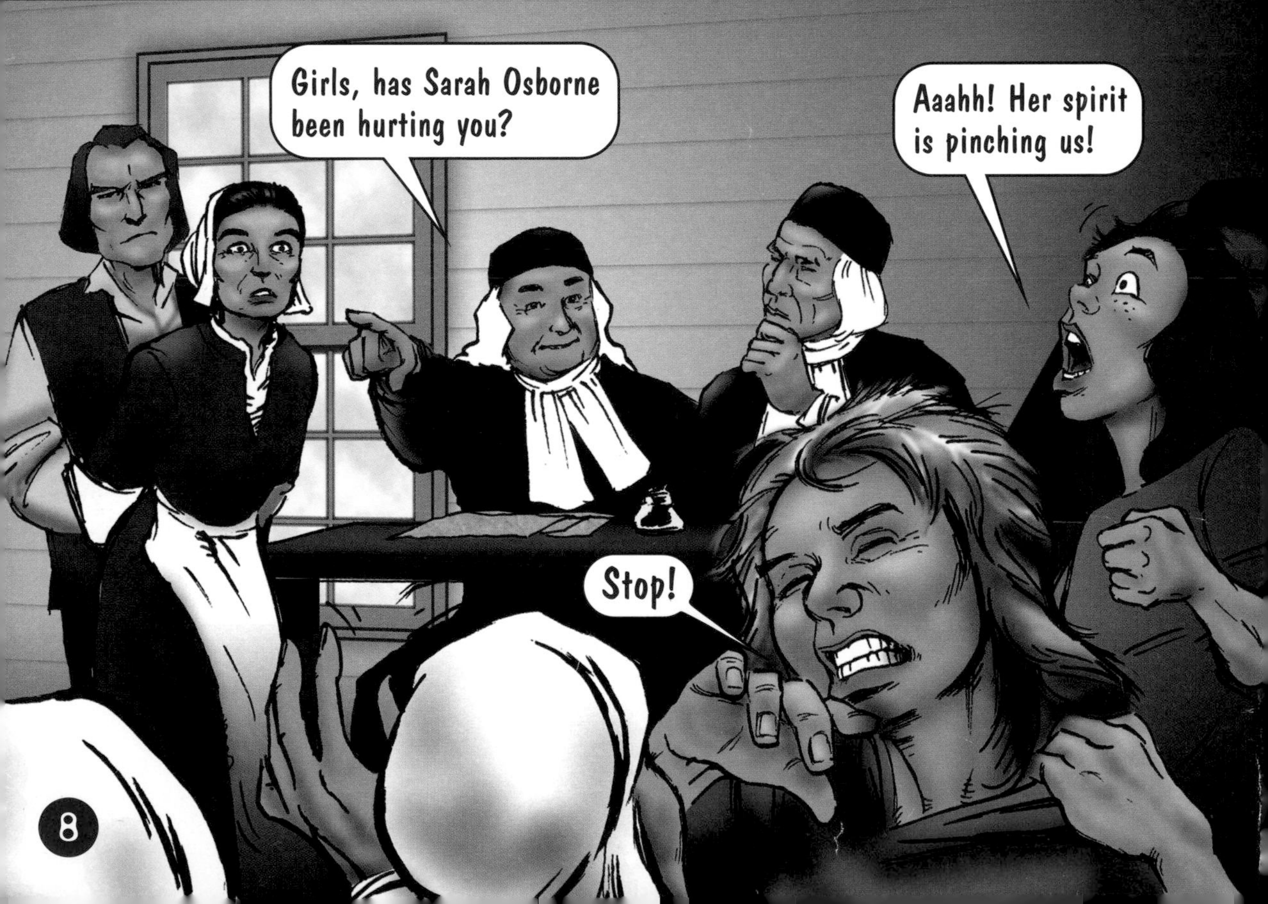
Girls, has Sarah Osborne been hurting you?
Aaahh! Her spirit is pinching us!
Stop!

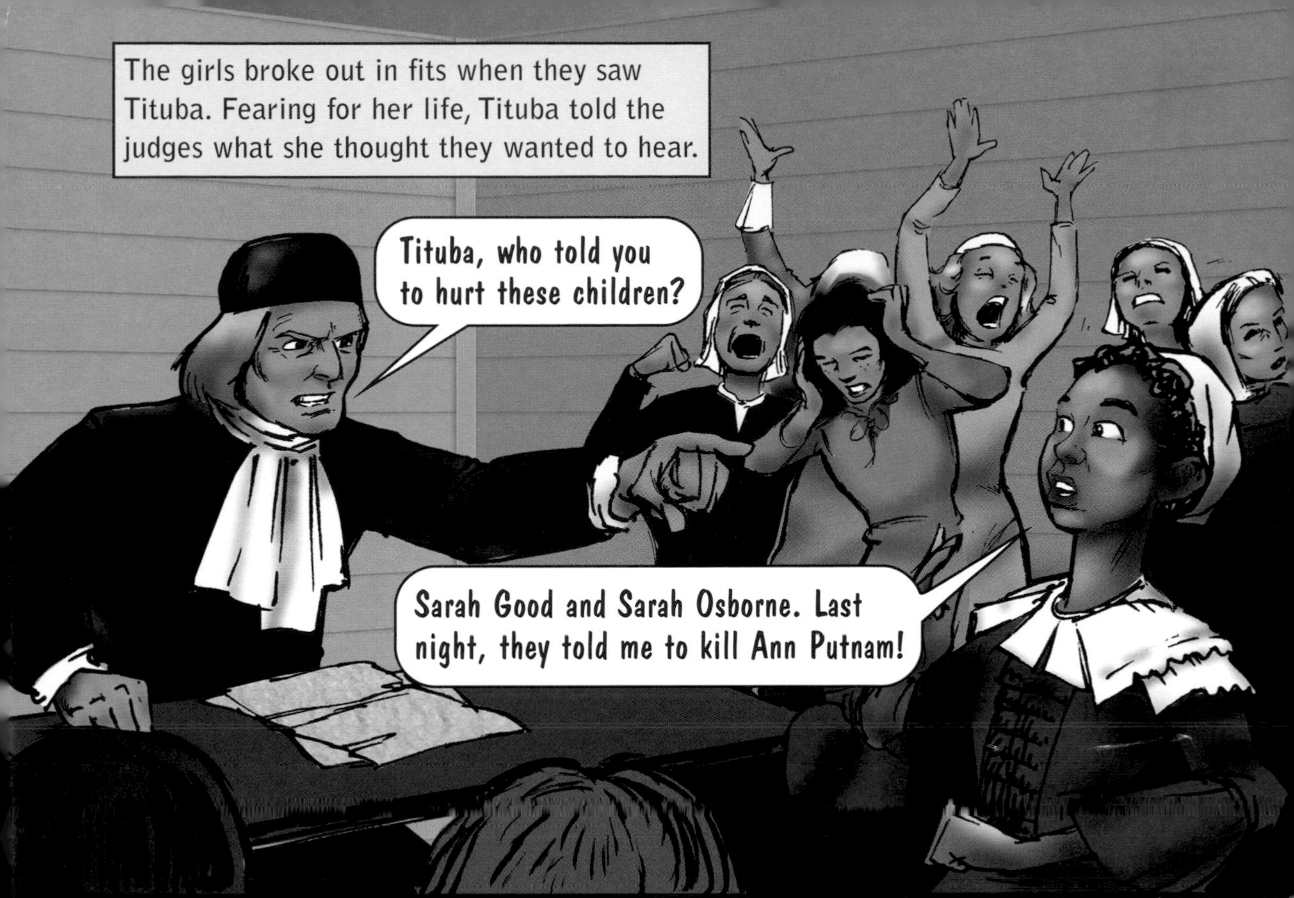
The girls broke out in fits when they saw Tituba. Fearing for her life, Tituba told the judges what she thought they wanted to hear.
Tituba, who told you to hurt these children?
Sarah Good and Sarah Osborne. Last night, they told me to kill Ann Putnam!

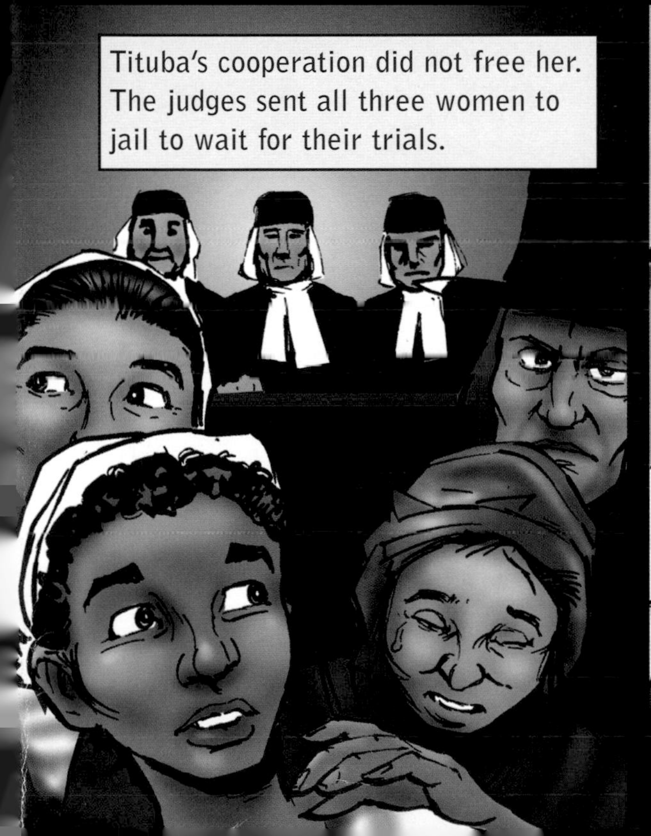
Tituba's cooperation did not free her. The judges sent all three women to jail to wait for their trials.

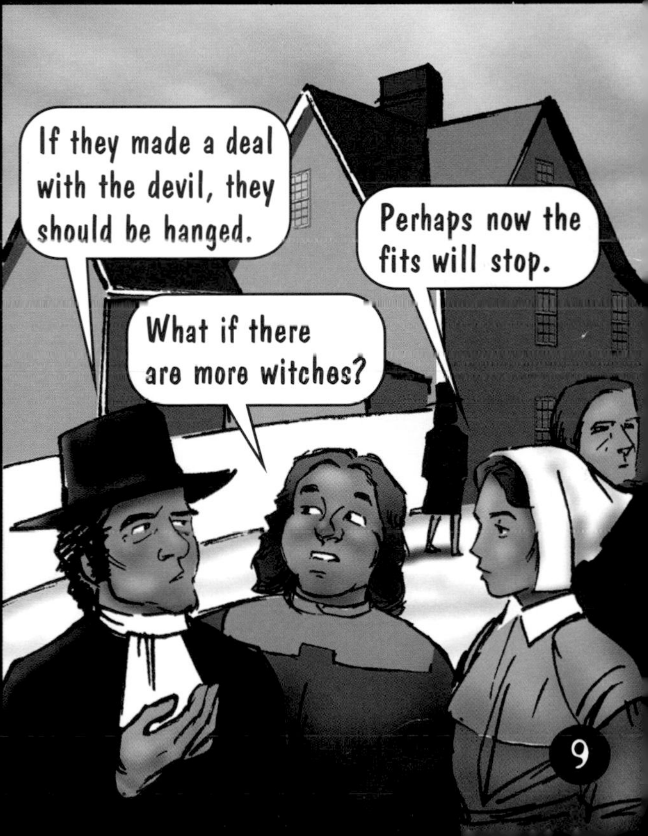
If they made a deal with the devil, they should be hanged.
Perhaps now the fits will stop.
What if there are more witches?

CHAPTER · 2

# More Accusations

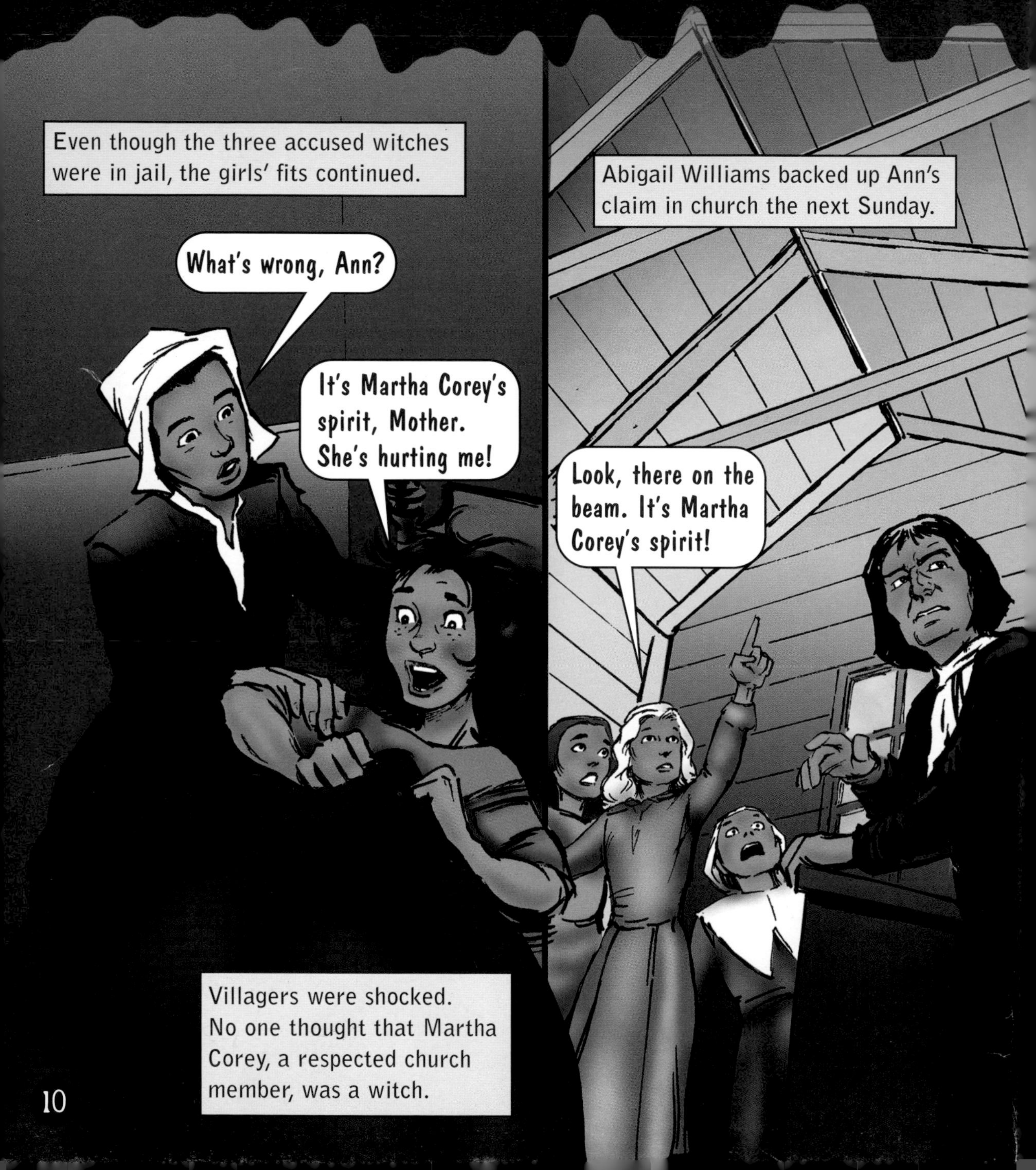
Even though the three accused witches were in jail, the girls' fits continued.
What's wrong, Ann?
It's Martha Corey's spirit, Mother. She's hurting me!
Villagers were shocked. No one thought that Martha Corey, a respected church member, was a witch.
Abigail Williams backed up Ann's claim in church the next Sunday.
Look, there on the beam. It's Martha Corey's spirit!

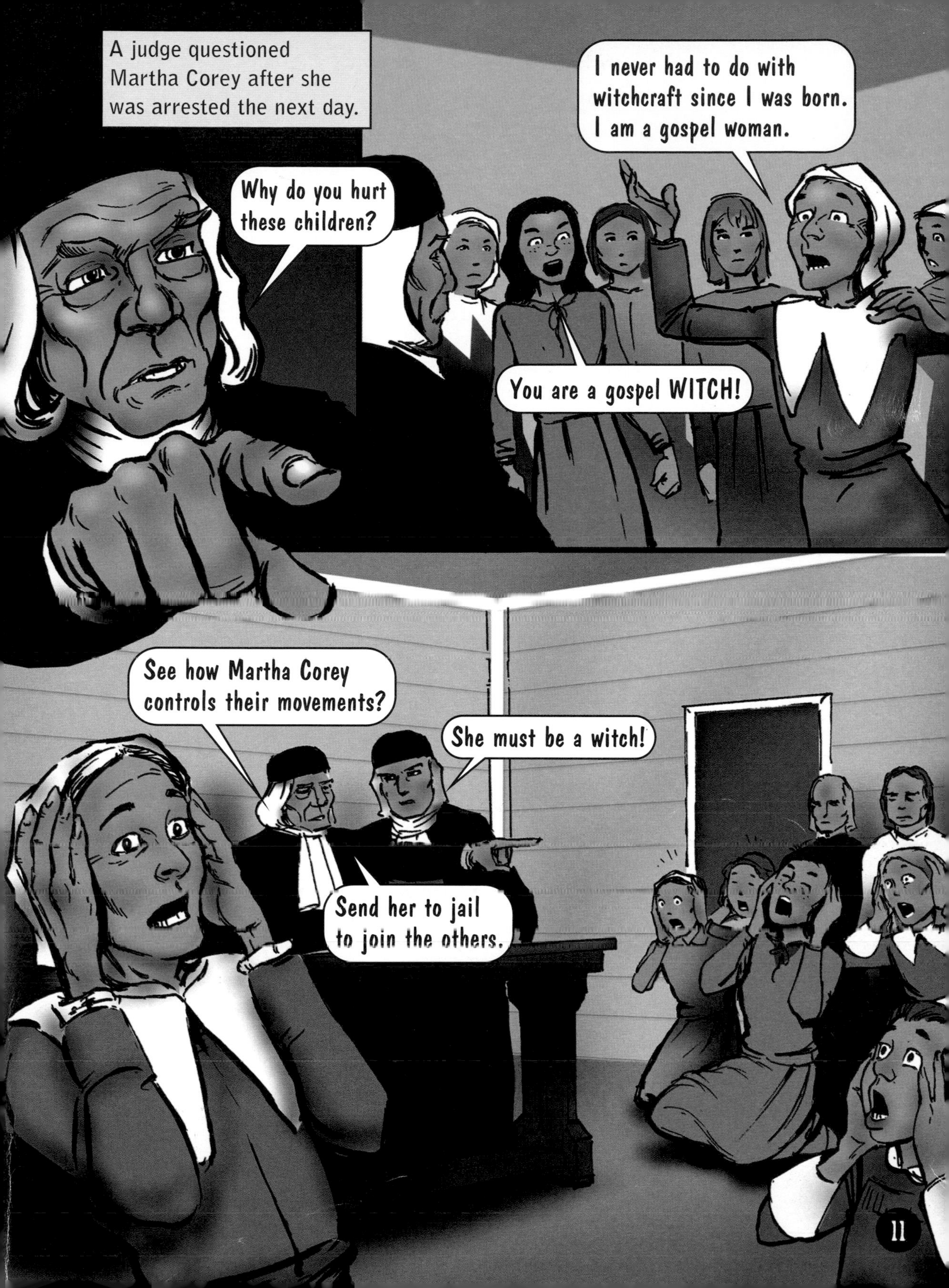

A judge questioned Martha Corey after she was arrested the next day.
Why do you hurt these children?
I never had to do with witchcraft since I was born. I am a gospel woman.
You are a gospel WITCH!
See how Martha Corey controls their movements?
She must be a witch!
Send her to jail to join the others.

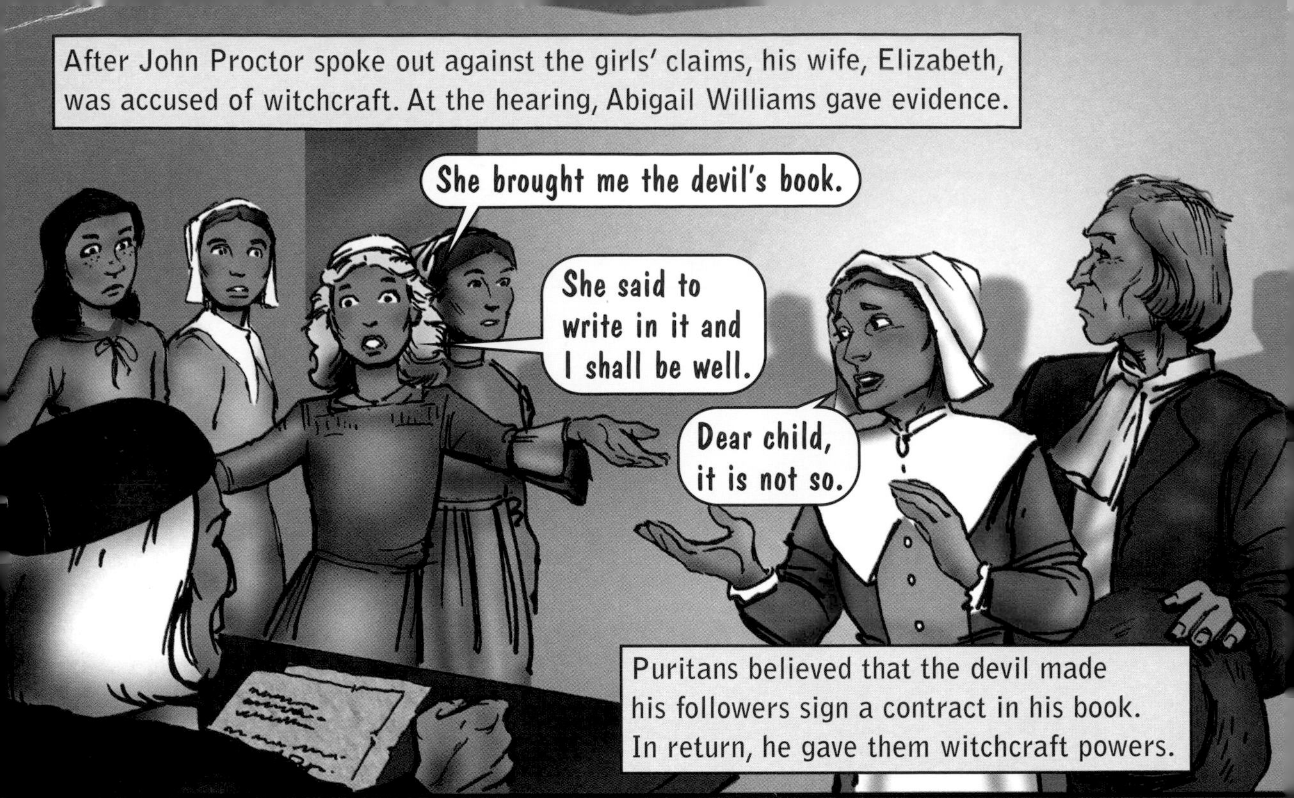
After John Proctor spoke out against the girls' claims, his wife, Elizabeth, was accused of witchcraft. At the hearing, Abigail Williams gave evidence.
She brought me the devil's book.
She said to write in it and I shall be well.
Dear child, it is not so.
Puritans believed that the devil made his followers sign a contract in his book. In return, he gave them witchcraft powers.

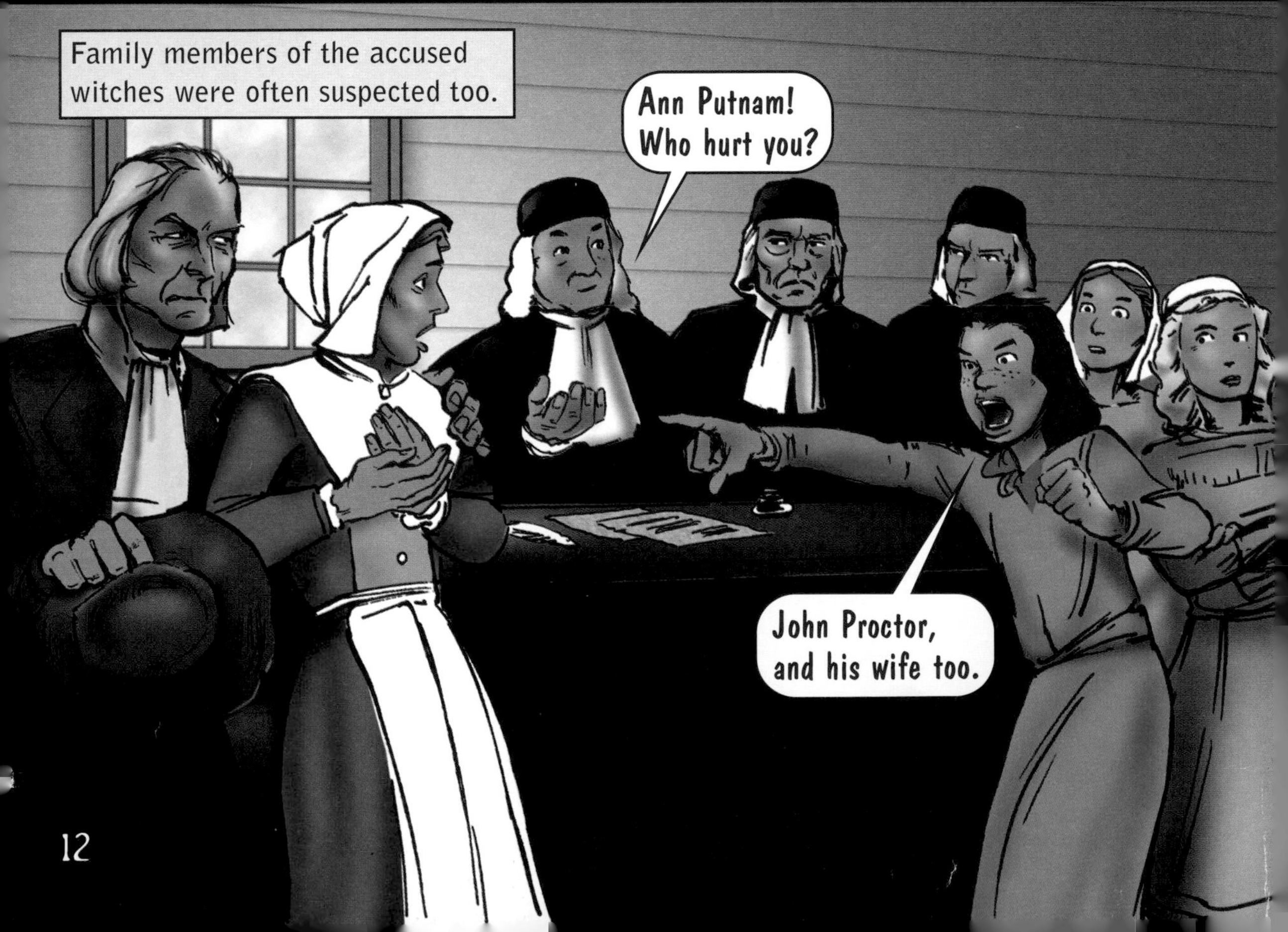
Family members of the accused witches were often suspected too.
Ann Putnam! Who hurt you?
John Proctor, and his wife too.

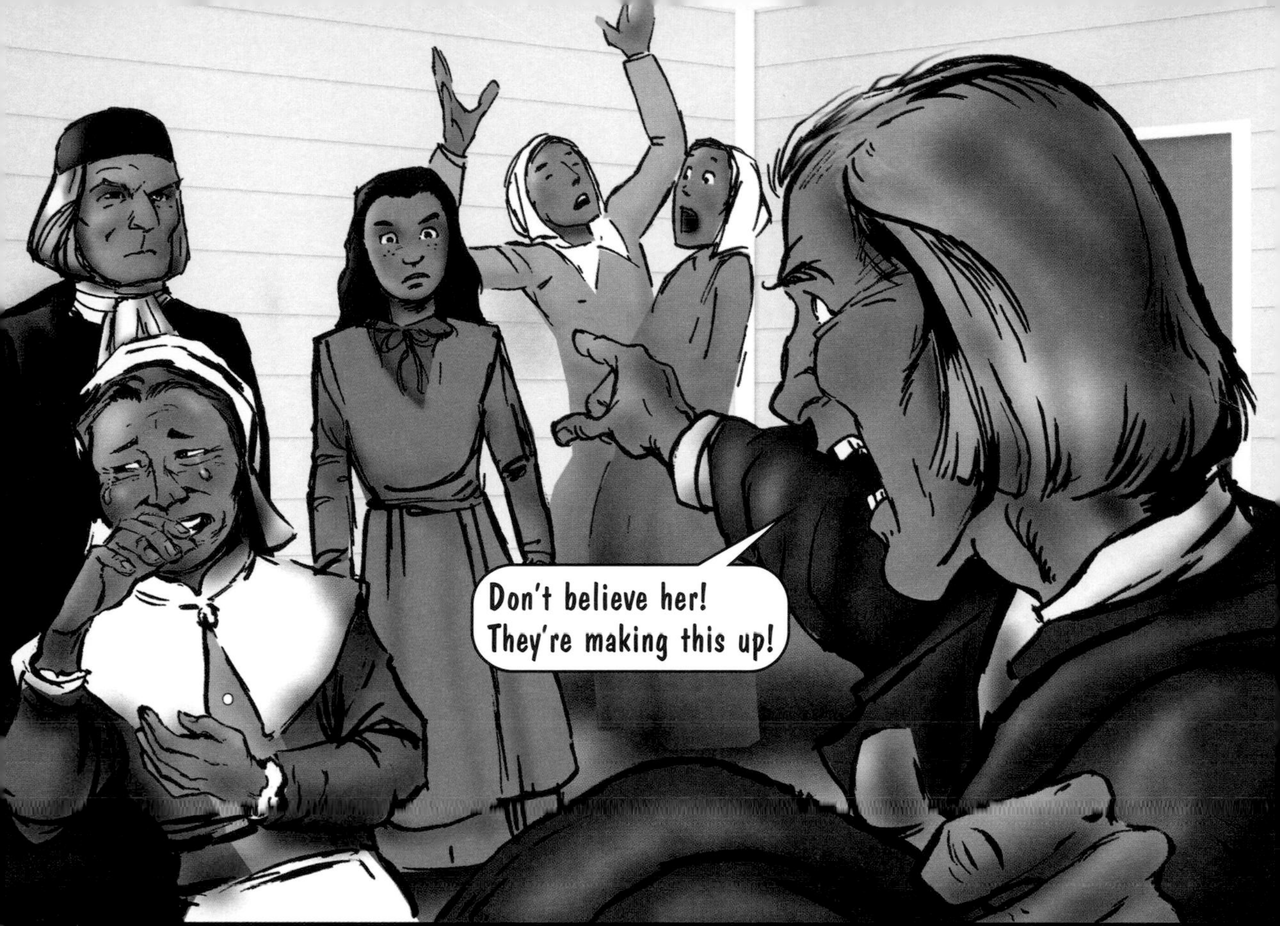
Don't believe her!
They're making this up!

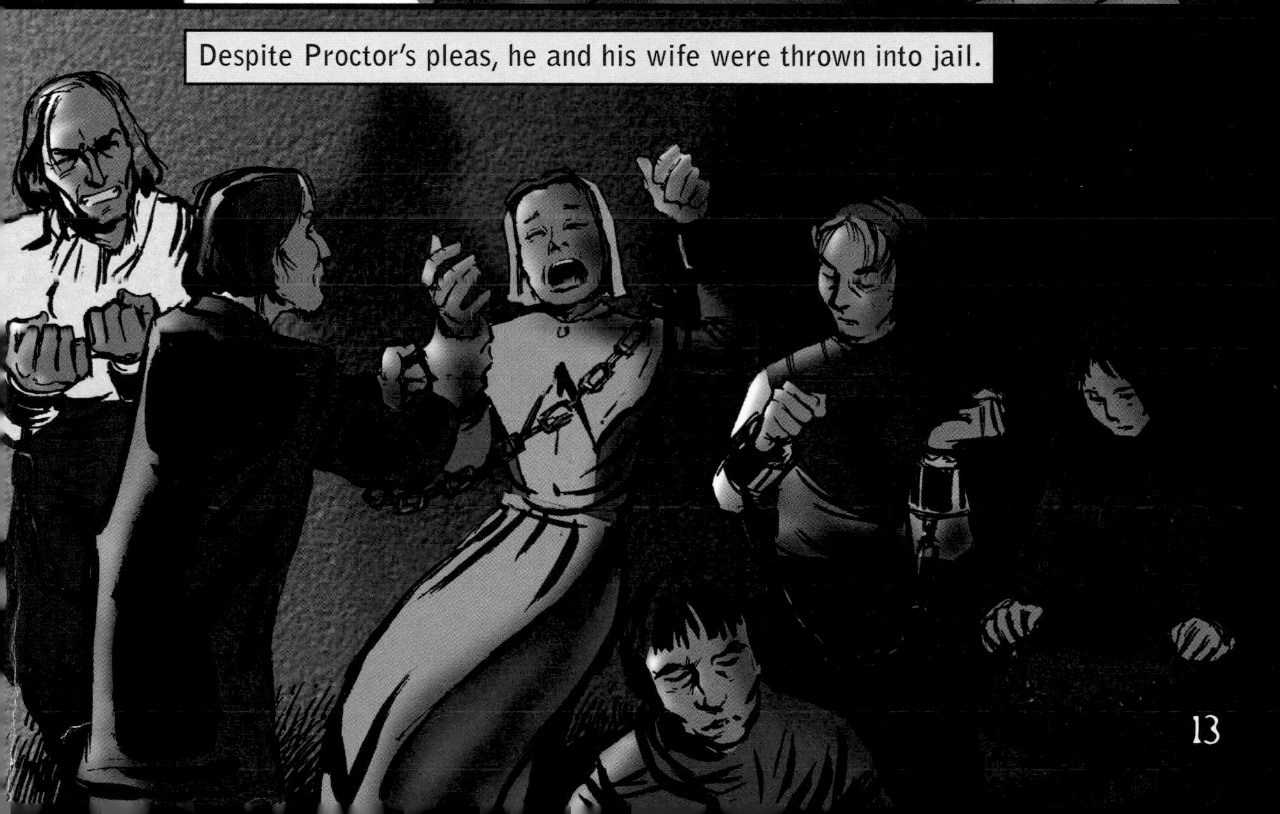
Despite Proctor's pleas, he and his wife were thrown into jail.

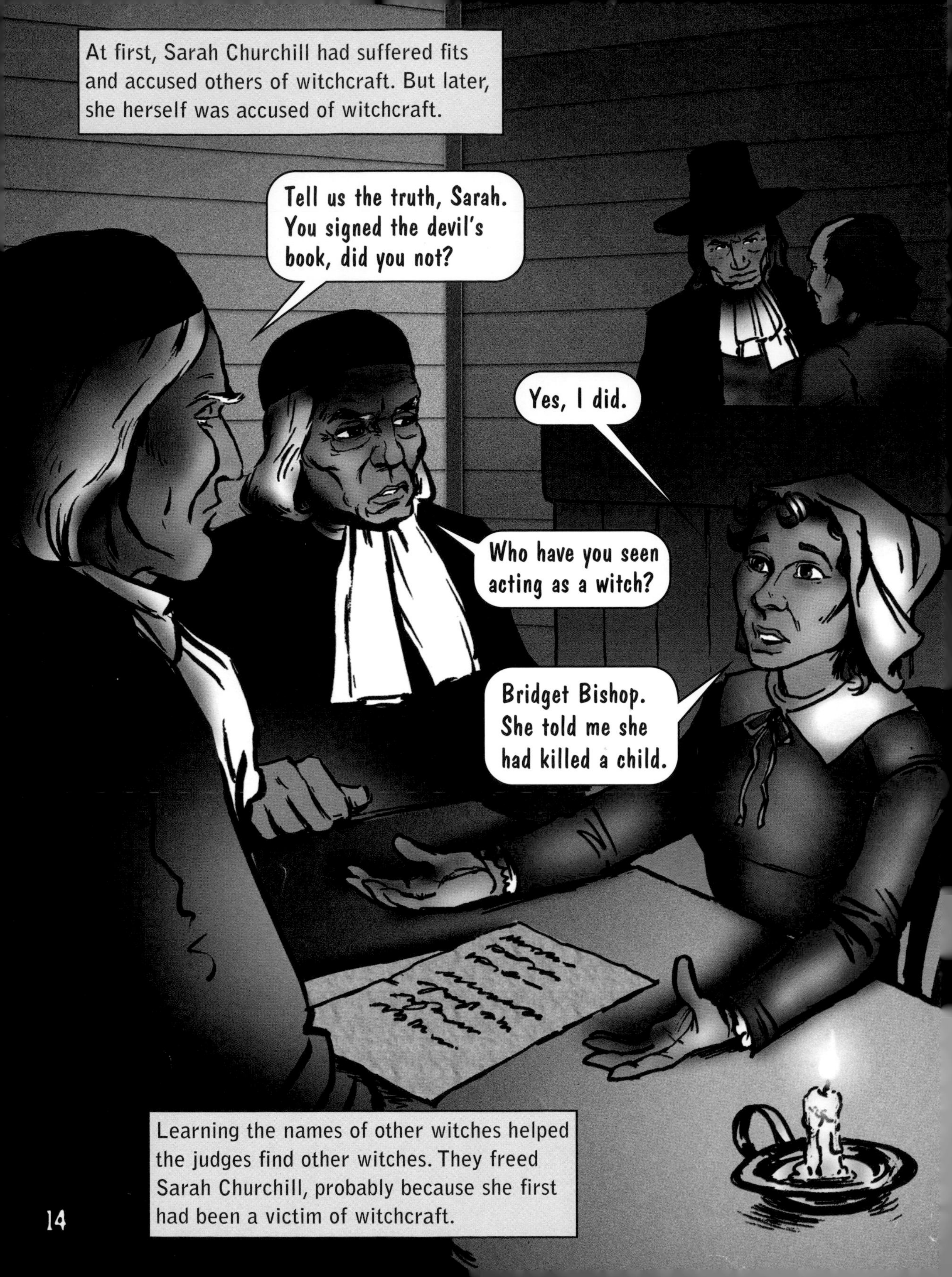
At first, Sarah Churchill had suffered fits and accused others of witchcraft. But later, she herself was accused of witchcraft.
Tell us the truth, Sarah. You signed the devil's book, did you not?
Yes, I did.
Who have you seen acting as a witch?
Bridget Bishop. She told me she had killed a child.
Learning the names of other witches helped the judges find other witches. They freed Sarah Churchill, probably because she first had been a victim of witchcraft.

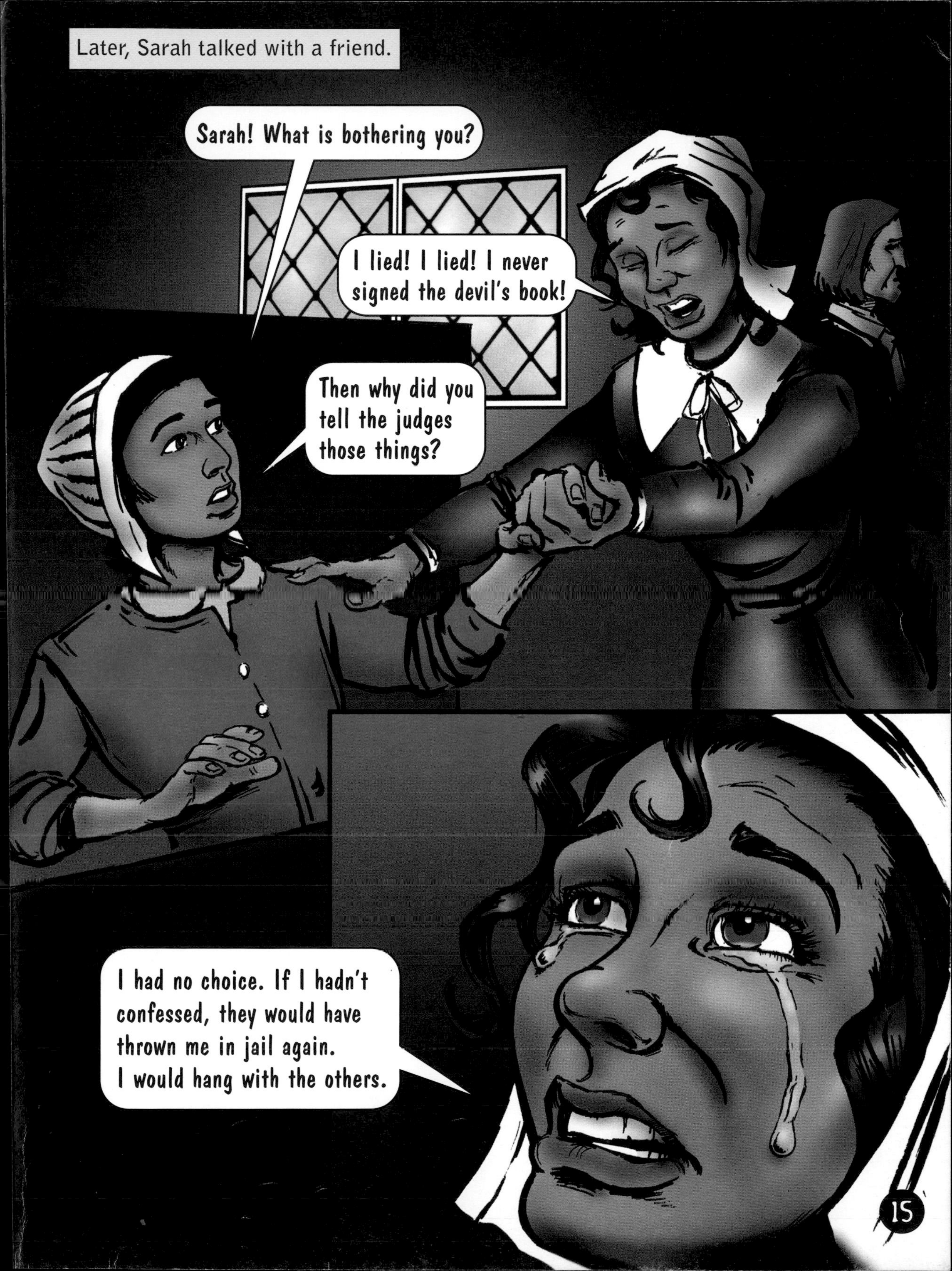
Later, Sarah talked with a friend.
Sarah! What is bothering you?
I lied! I lied! I never signed the devil's book!
Then why did you tell the judges those things?
I had no choice. If I hadn't confessed, they would have thrown me in jail again. I would hang with the others.

CHAPTER · 3

# The Trials

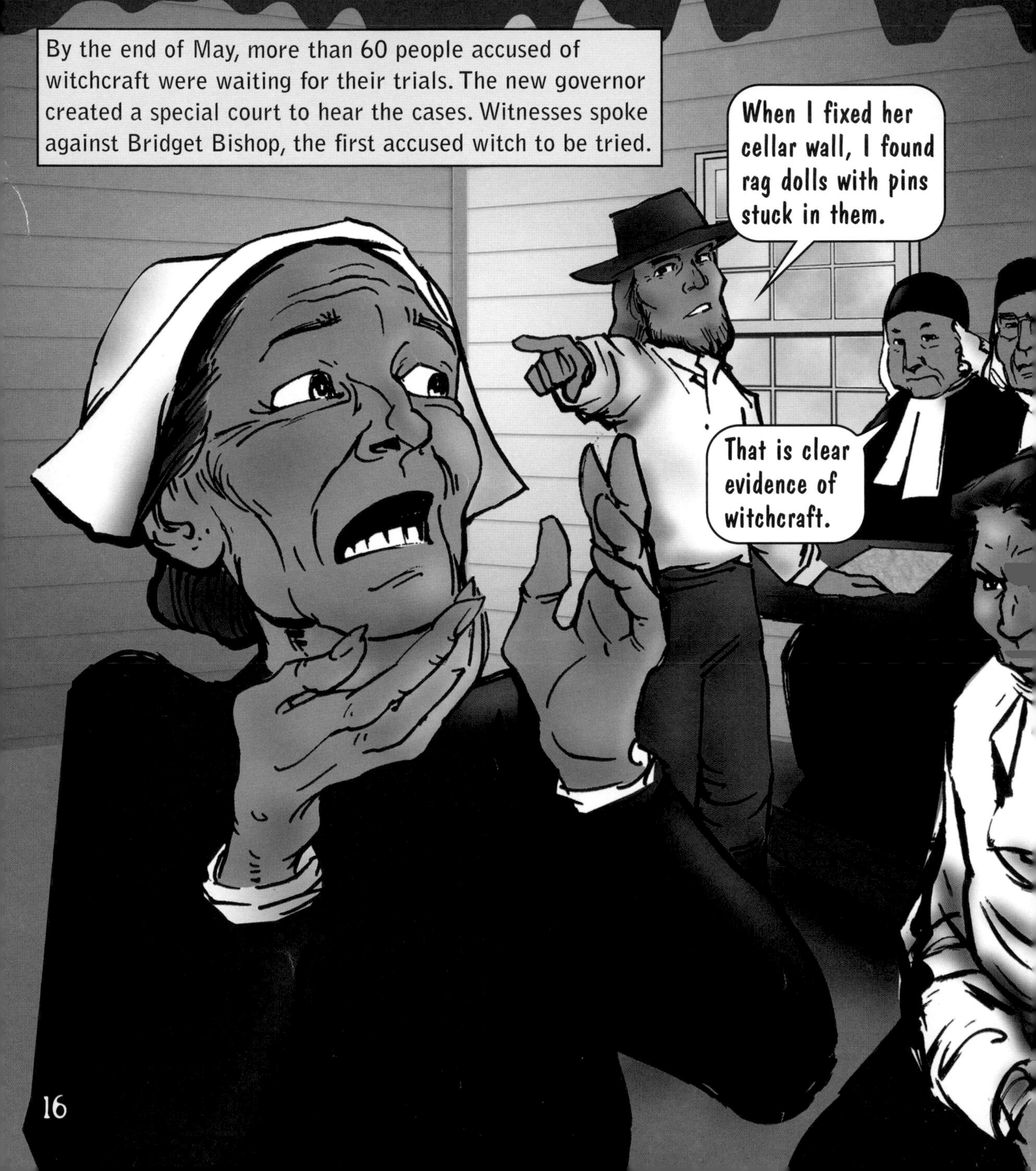
By the end of May, more than 60 people accused of witchcraft were waiting for their trials. The new governor created a special court to hear the cases. Witnesses spoke against Bridget Bishop, the first accused witch to be tried.
When I fixed her cellar wall, I found rag dolls with pins stuck in them.
That is clear evidence of witchcraft.

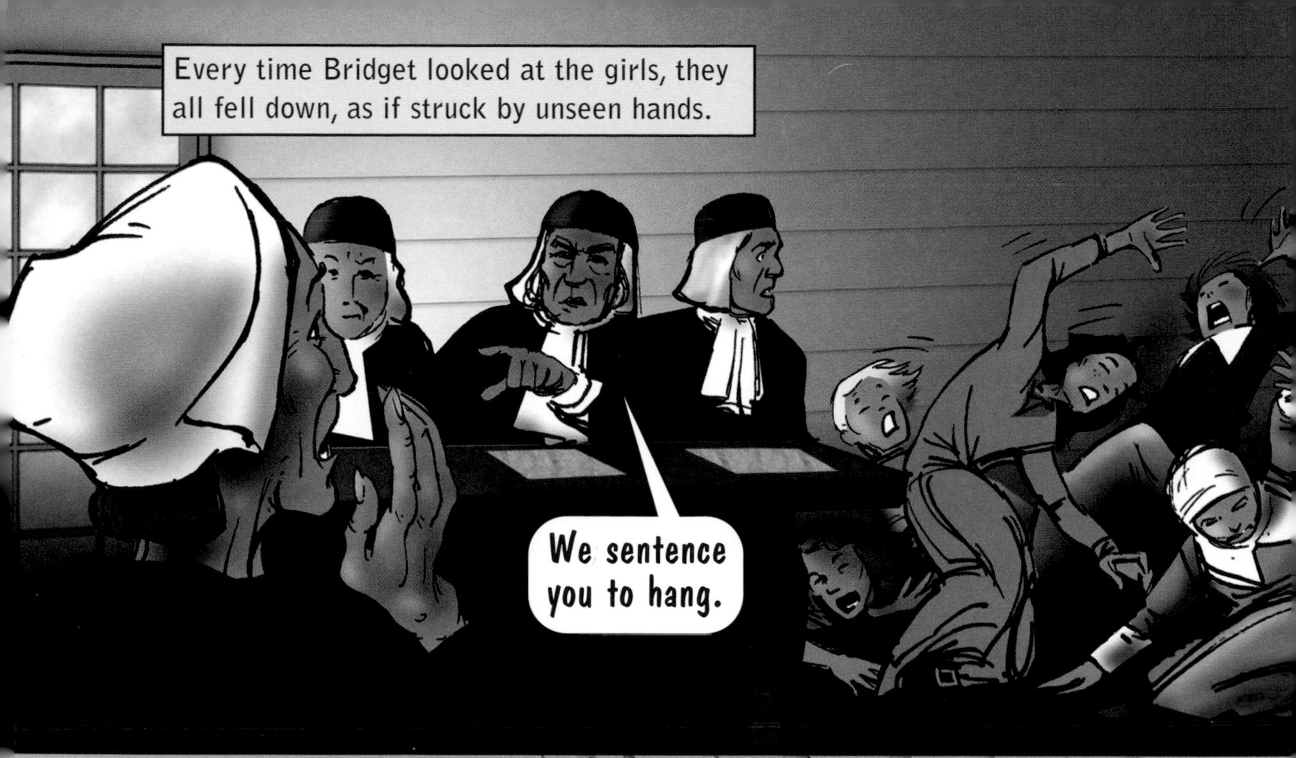
Every time Bridget looked at the girls, they all fell down, as if struck by unseen hands.
We sentence you to hang.

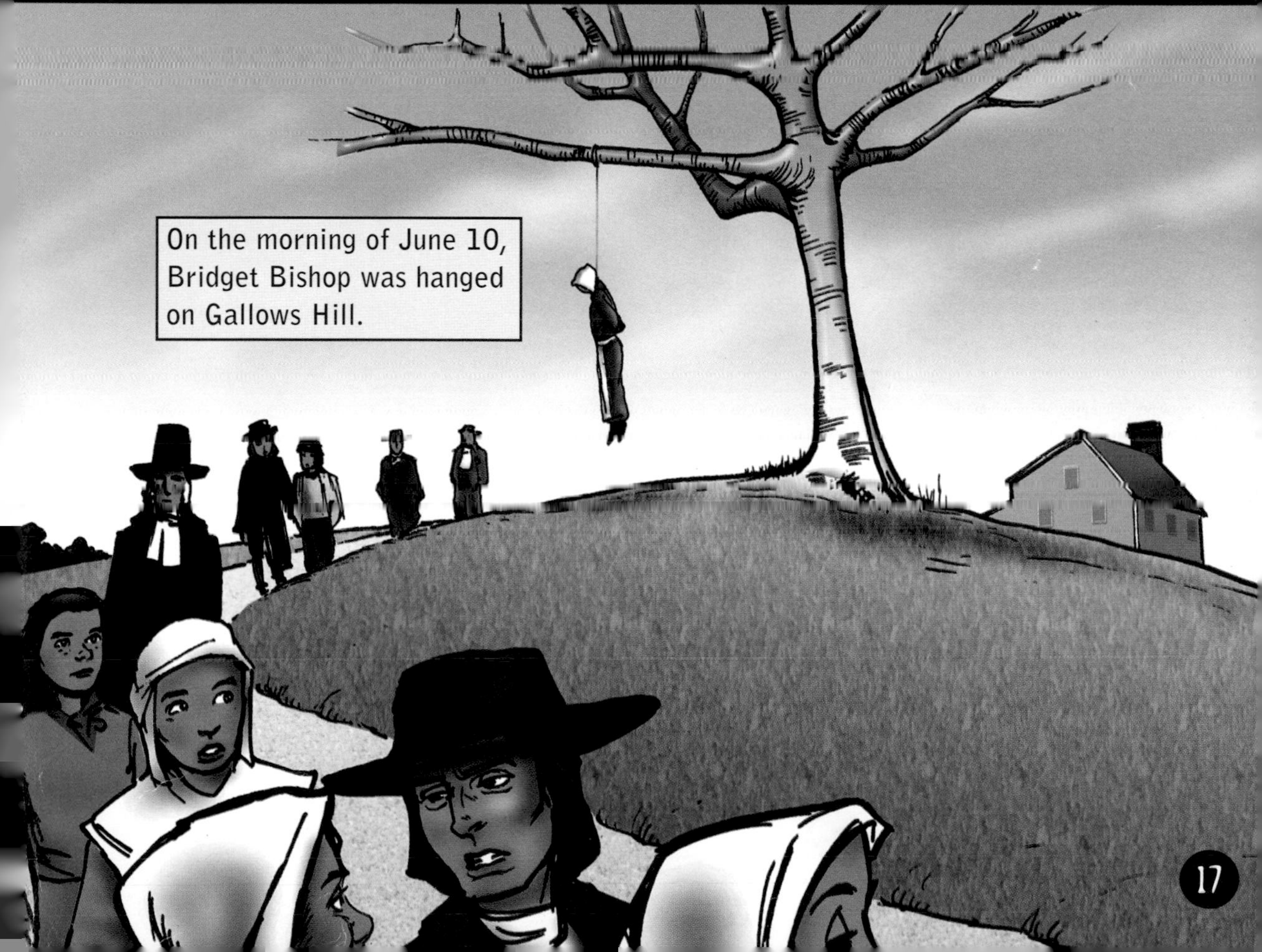
On the morning of June 10, Bridget Bishop was hanged on Gallows Hill.

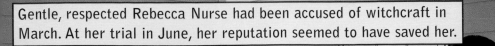

Gentle, respected Rebecca Nurse had been accused of witchcraft in March. At her trial in June, her reputation seemed to have saved her.

We find Rebecca Nurse innocent of witchcraft.

No! No! No!

Make her stop! She's choking me!

Please don't let her go! Can't you see she's hurting us?

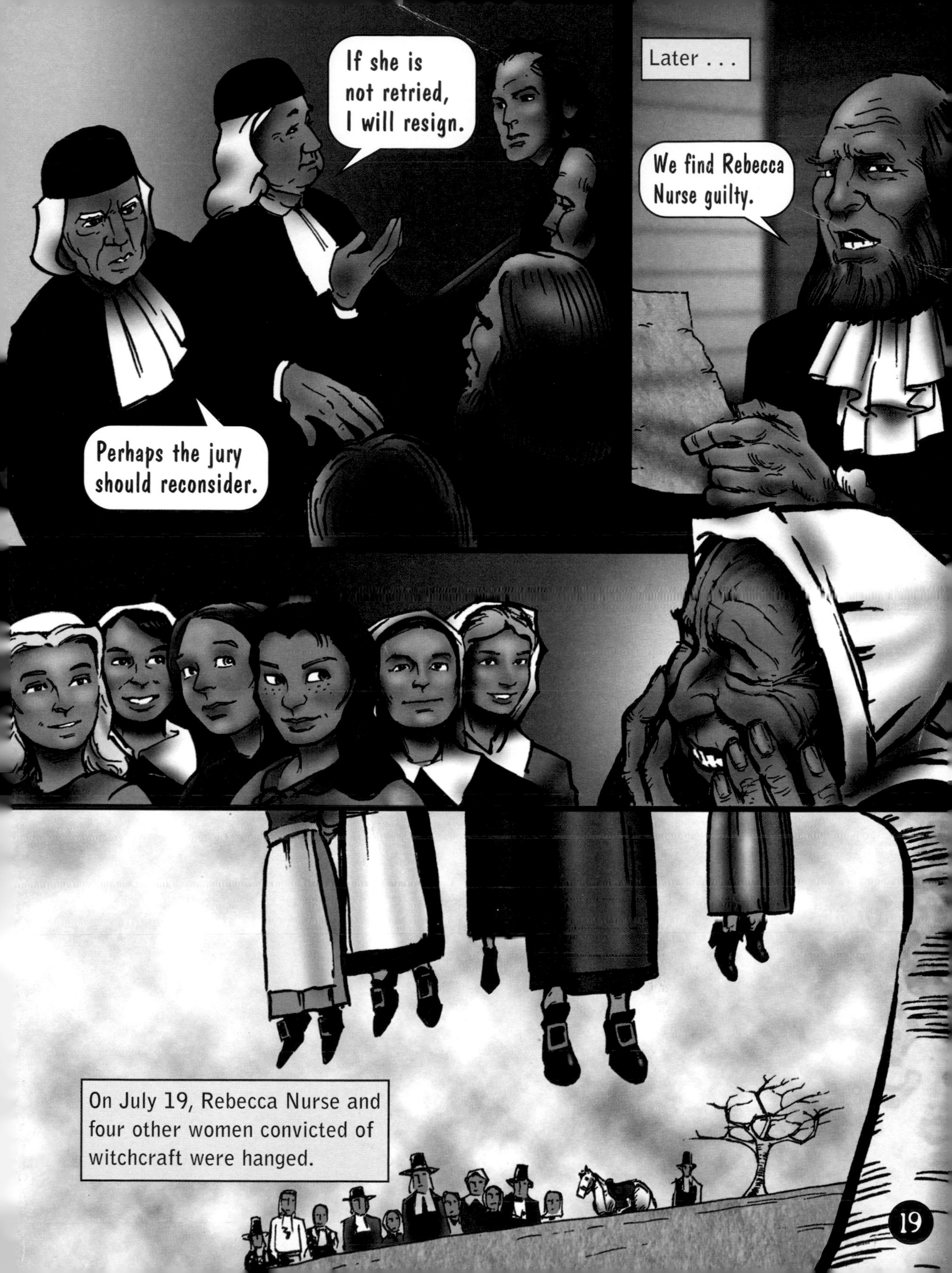

If she is not retried, I will resign.
Perhaps the jury should reconsider.
Later . . .
We find Rebecca Nurse guilty.
On July 19, Rebecca Nurse and four other women convicted of witchcraft were hanged.

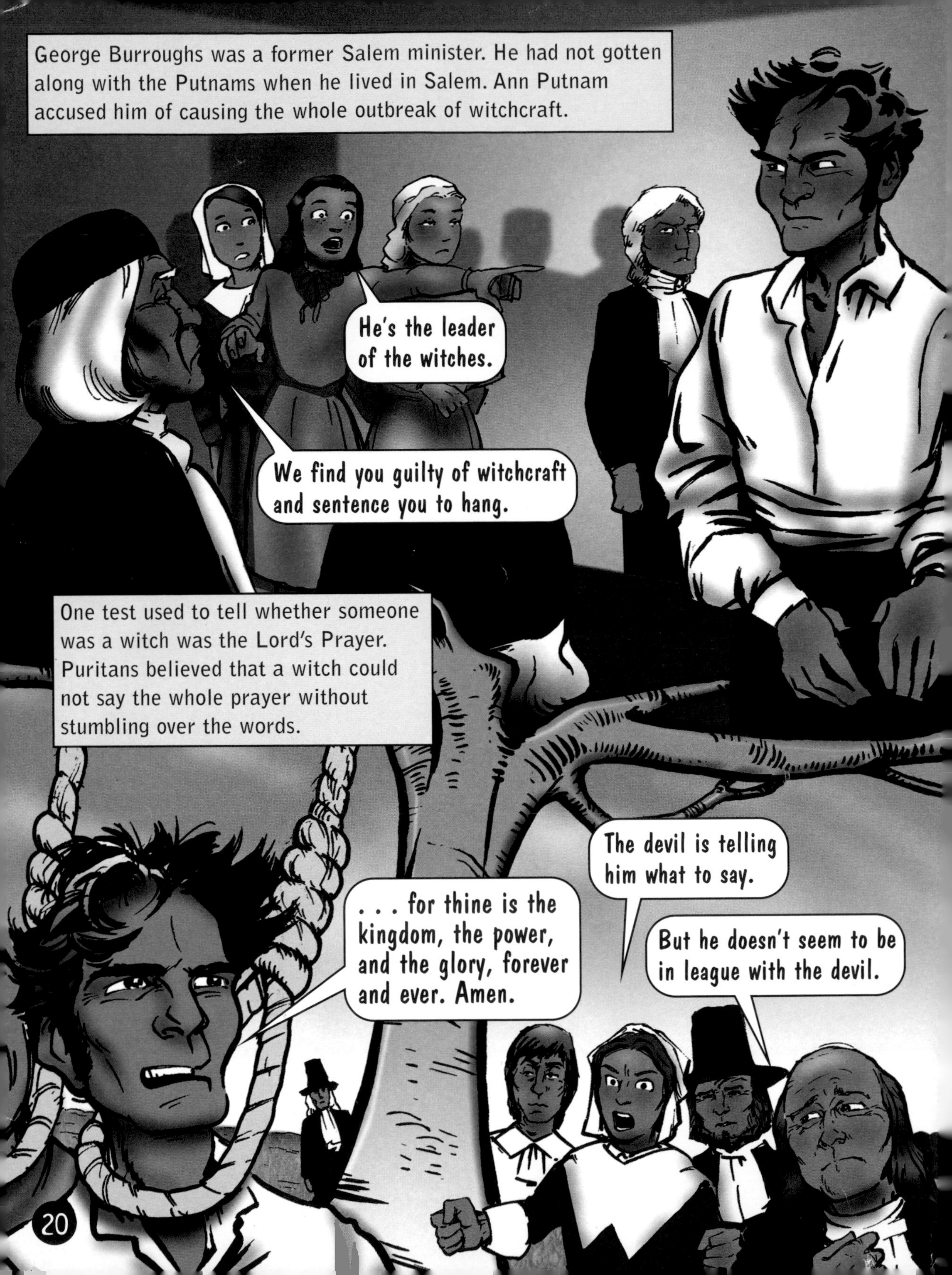
George Burroughs was a former Salem minister. He had not gotten along with the Putnams when he lived in Salem. Ann Putnam accused him of causing the whole outbreak of witchcraft.
He's the leader of the witches.
We find you guilty of witchcraft and sentence you to hang.
One test used to tell whether someone was a witch was the Lord's Prayer. Puritans believed that a witch could not say the whole prayer without stumbling over the words.
. . . for thine is the kingdom, the power, and the glory, forever and ever. Amen.
The devil is telling him what to say.
But he doesn't seem to be in league with the devil.

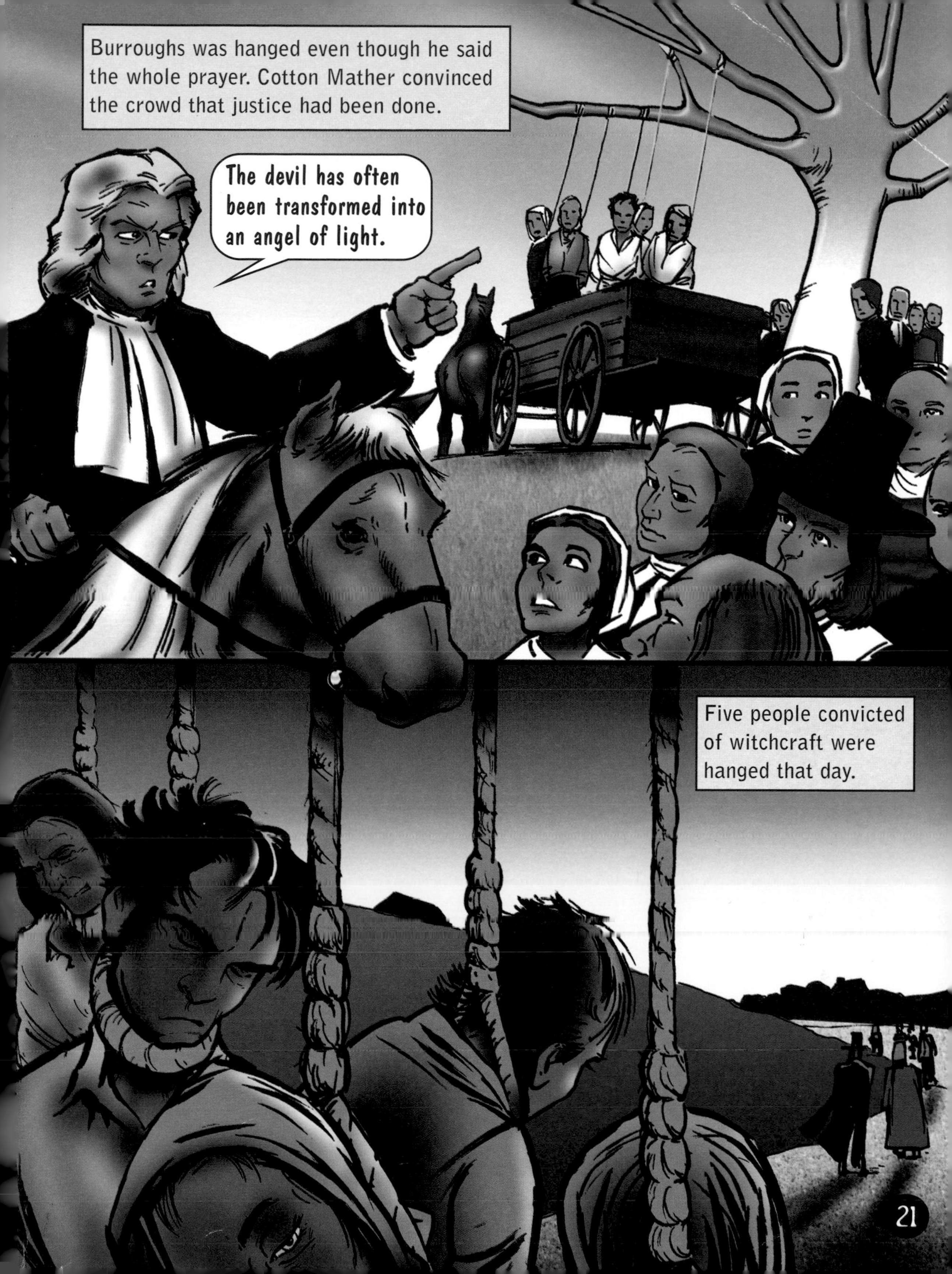
Burroughs was hanged even though he said the whole prayer. Cotton Mather convinced the crowd that justice had been done.
The devil has often been transformed into an angel of light.
Five people convicted of witchcraft were hanged that day.

CHAPTER · 4

# Witchcraft Hysteria

Fear gripped New England, creating mass hysteria. Whenever anyone got sick, witchcraft was suspected. People in nearby towns looked for witches too. They sent for the girls from Salem.

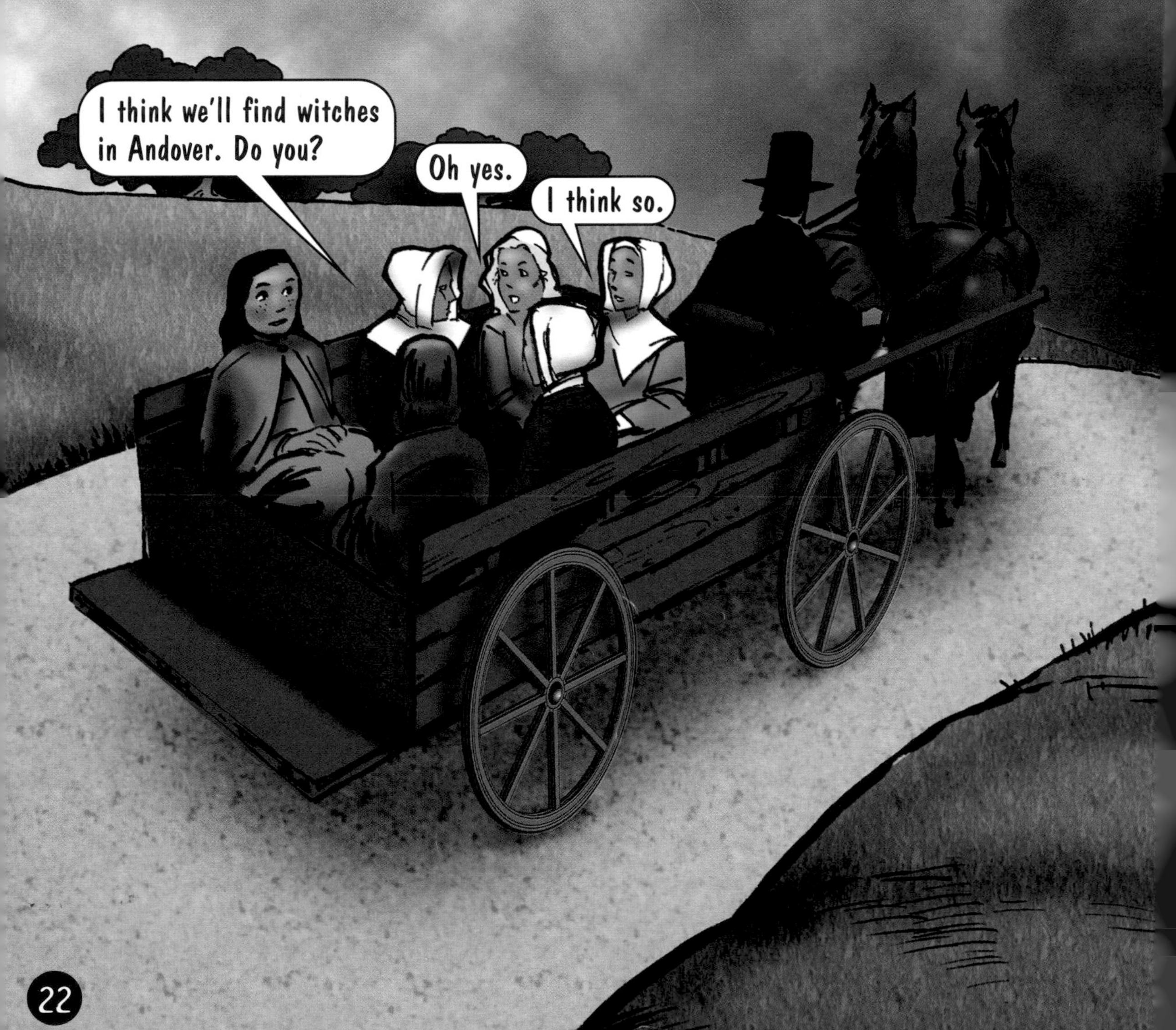
I think we'll find witches in Andover. Do you?
Oh yes.
I think so.

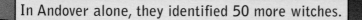

In Andover alone, they identified 50 more witches.

Is this man making Joseph Ballard's wife sick?

Yes, the devil is whispering in his ear. He's doing Satan's work.

People like Reverend Parris talked of an all-out battle between good and evil.

The devil will be making war with the lamb and his followers as long as he can.

Others were beginning to wonder about the accusers.

How can they accuse people they don't even know?

What if the devil is making them accuse innocent people?

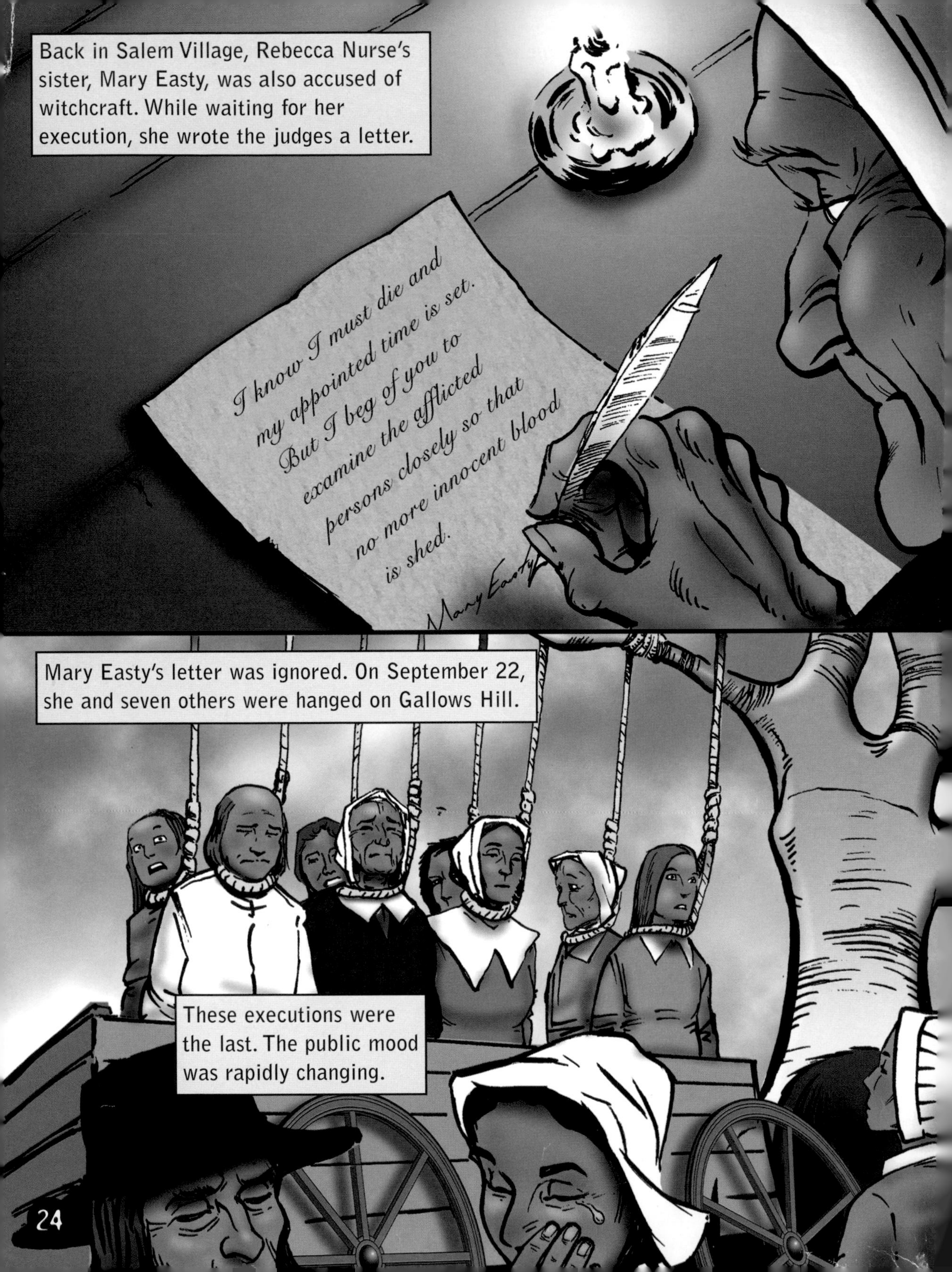
Back in Salem Village, Rebecca Nurse's sister, Mary Easty, was also accused of witchcraft. While waiting for her execution, she wrote the judges a letter.
I know I must die and my appointed time is set. But I beg of you to examine the afflicted persons closely so that no more innocent blood is shed.
Mary Easty
Mary Easty's letter was ignored. On September 22, she and seven others were hanged on Gallows Hill.
These executions were the last. The public mood was rapidly changing.

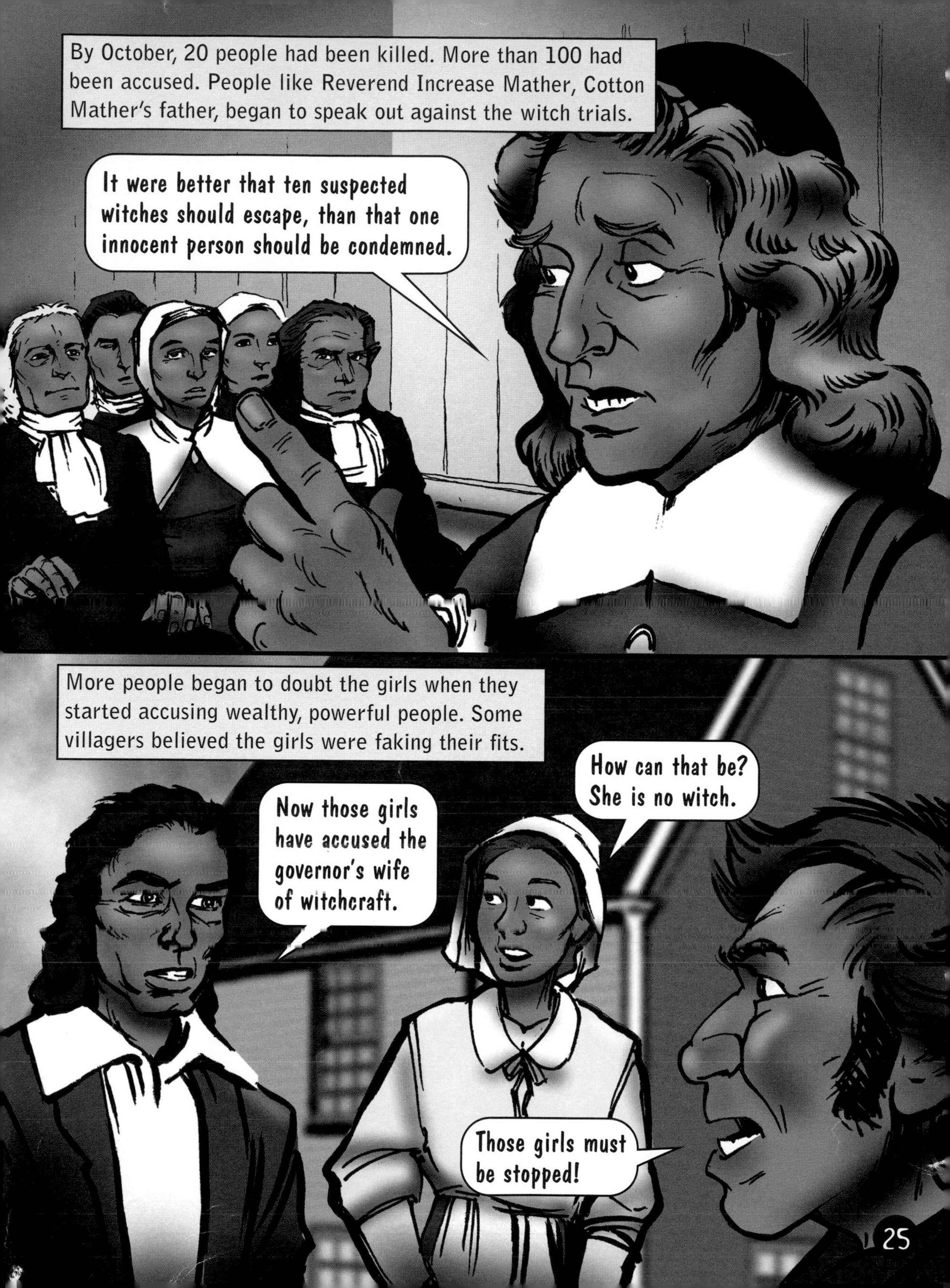
By October, 20 people had been killed. More than 100 had been accused. People like Reverend Increase Mather, Cotton Mather's father, began to speak out against the witch trials.
It were better that ten suspected witches should escape, than that one innocent person should be condemned.
More people began to doubt the girls when they started accusing wealthy, powerful people. Some villagers believed the girls were faking their fits.
Now those girls have accused the governor's wife of witchcraft.
How can that be? She is no witch.
Those girls must be stopped!

On October 12, Governor William Phipps made an announcement.
From this day forward, no accused witches shall be sent to jail until they are found guilty by a court.

The following spring, Governor Phipps ended the witch trials for good.
The governor has freed all accused witches.
We are saved!

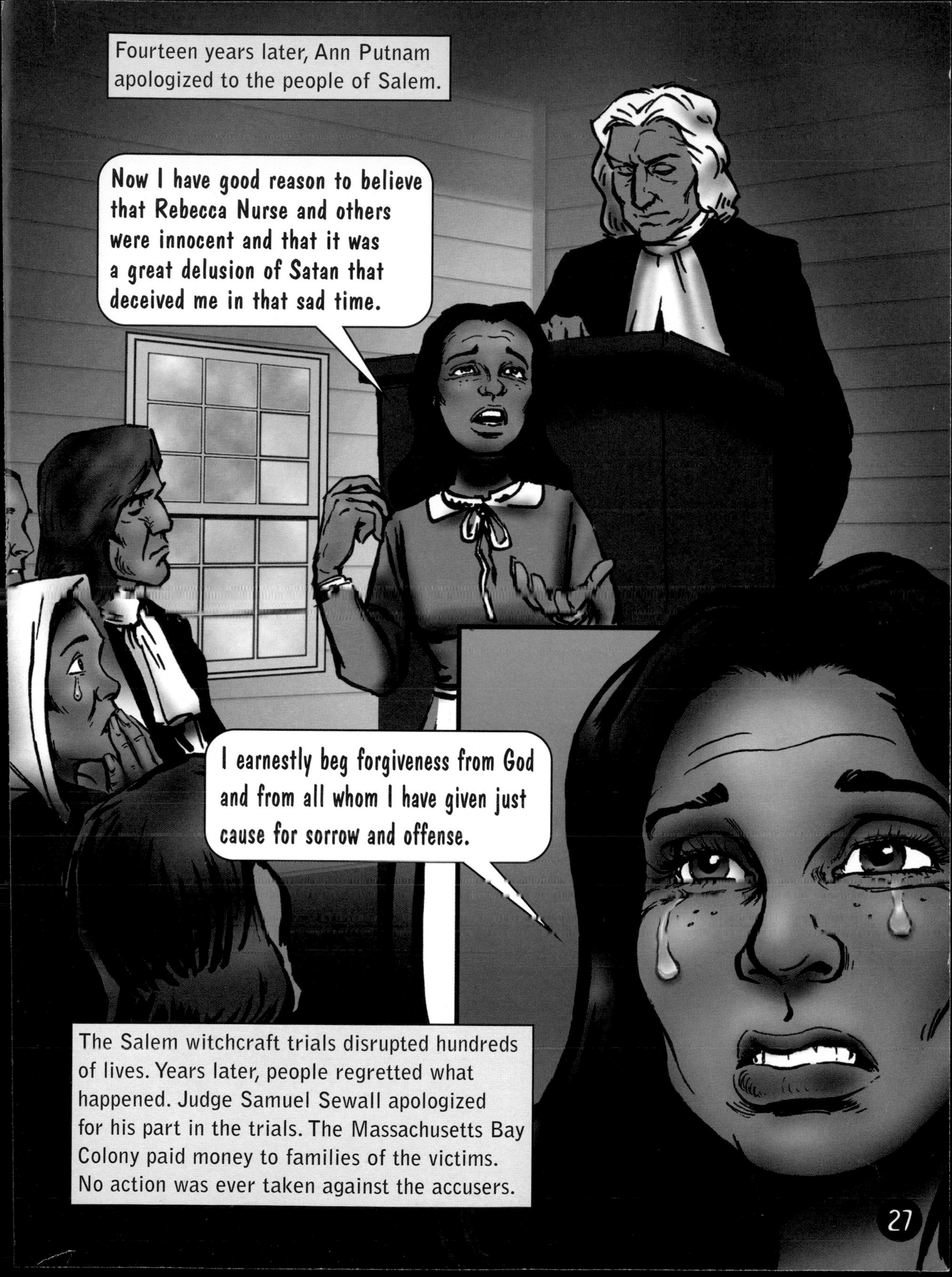
Fourteen years later, Ann Putnam apologized to the people of Salem.
Now I have good reason to believe that Rebecca Nurse and others were innocent and that it was a great delusion of Satan that deceived me in that sad time.
I earnestly beg forgiveness from God and from all whom I have given just cause for sorrow and offense.
The Salem witchcraft trials disrupted hundreds of lives. Years later, people regretted what happened. Judge Samuel Sewall apologized for his part in the trials. The Massachusetts Bay Colony paid money to families of the victims. No action was ever taken against the accusers.

# The Salem Witch Trials

✳ **Salem Witch Trials Statistics**

| | |
|---|---:|
| Number of accusers: | 19 |
| Number of people arrested as witches: | about 150 |
| Number of arrested people convicted: | 28 |
| Number of convicted people hanged: | 19 |
| Other deaths: | 4 died in jail |
| | 1 man pressed to death |

✳ **Dates of Hangings**

| | |
|---|---|
| June 10, 1692 | Bridget Bishop |
| July 19, 1692 | Sarah Good, Elizabeth Howe, Susannah Martin, Rebecca Nurse, and Sarah Wilds |
| August 19, 1692 | Reverend George Burroughs, Martha Carrier, George Jacobs, John Proctor, and John Willard |
| September 22, 1692 | Martha Corey, Mary Easty, Alice Parker, Mary Parker, Ann Pudeator, Wilmot Redd, Margaret Scott, and Samuel Wardwell |

## The Theories

For more than 300 years, historians have tried to explain what caused the witchcraft outbreak in Salem in 1692.

- Writing shortly after the trials, Robert Calef thought the accusers were faking their acts. He blamed ministers like Cotton Mather for creating a climate of mass hysteria.

- Historians Paul Boyer and Stephen Nissenbaum believe that power struggles and family feuds made people accuse others of witchcraft.

- Laurie Winn Carlson, a historian, believed that a disease called encephalitis caused the girls' fits. The disease, spread by mosquitoes, can cause fever, confusion, and seizures.

- Chadwick Hansen thought that some people in Salem really did practice witchcraft, and people were very afraid of it.

- Bernard Rosenthal offered several reasons that the stories of witchcraft were made up. His reasons included jealousy, getting rid of personal enemies, and people truly believing in witches.

- A recent historian, Mary Beth Norton, blamed the climate of fear on wars with American Indians. When the wars began going badly, fearful New Englanders searching for a reason blamed witchcraft.

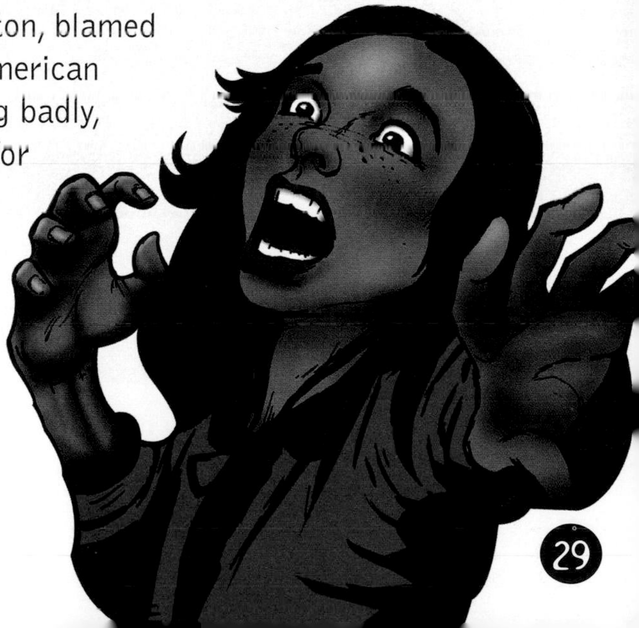

# Glossary

**afflicted** (uh-FLIK-ted)—being affected by a disease or condition, such as witchcraft

**execution** (ek-suh-KYOO-shuhn)—the act of putting someone to death as punishment for a crime

**hearing** (HIHR-ing)—a meeting held by judges to see if there is enough evidence to hold a trial

**Lord's Prayer** (LORDZ PRAY-ur)—a prayer said by Christians; this prayer appears in the Bible.

**mass hysteria** (MASS hiss-TEHR-ee-uh)—overwhelming fear or panic felt by many people at one time

**Puritans** (PYOOR-uh-tuhns)—a group of Protestants in England during the 1500s and 1600s who wanted simple church services and enforced a strict moral code; many Puritans fled England and settled in North America.

# Internet Sites

FactHound offers a safe, fun way to find Internet sites related to this book. All of the sites on FactHound have been researched by our staff.

Here's how:

1. Visit *www.facthound.com*
2. Type in this special code **0736838473** for age-appropriate sites. Or enter a search word related to this book for a more general search.
3. Click on the **Fetch It** button.

FactHound will fetch the best sites for you!

# Read More

Aronson, Marc. *Witch-hunt: Mysteries of the Salem Witch Trials.* New York: Atheneum Books for Young Readers, 2003.

Boraas, Tracey. *The Salem Witch Trials.* Let Freedom Ring. Mankato, Minn.: Capstone Press, 2004.

Lutz, Norma Jean. *Cotton Mather.* Colonial Leaders. Philadelphia: Chelsea House, 2000.

Somervill, Barbara. *The Massachusetts Colony.* Our Thirteen Colonies. Chanhassen, Minn.: Child's World, 2004.

# Bibliography

Boyer, Paul, and Stephen Nissenbaum, eds. *The Salem Witchcraft Papers: Verbatim Transcripts of the Legal Documents of the Salem Witchcraft Outbreak of 1692.* University of Virginia Library, 2003. http://etext.virginia.edu/salem/witchcraft/texts/transcripts.html.

Hill, Frances. *A Delusion of Satan: The Full Story of the Salem Witch Trials.* New York: Doubleday, 1995.

Mather, Cotton. *Memorable Providences Relating to Witchcraft and Possession.* Edinburgh, 1697.

Norton, Mary Beth. *In the Devil's Snare: The Salem Witchcraft Crisis of 1692.* New York: Alfred A. Knopf, 2002.

Starkey, Marion Lena. *The Devil in Massachusetts: A Modern Inquiry into the Salem Witch Trials.* New York: Alfred A. Knopf, 1949. Reprinted with introduction by Aldous Huxley. Alexandria, Va.: Time-Life Books, 1982.

# Index

RIDGEFIELD LIBRARY